# THERE'S A SONG FOR THAT

## Lessons Learned from Music and Lyrics
## A Music Therapist's Memoir and Guide

JULIE HOFFER

There's A Song For That



ISBN 978-1-66783-177-0

eBook ISBN 978-1-66783-178-7

*For anyone who breaks into song anytime, anywhere,*
*with anyone…no apologies.*

CONTENTS

# I. OVERTURE

*"Listen to the music of the moment people dance and sing. We're just one big family, and it's our Godforsaken right to be loved." —Jason Mraz*

Are you ready to rock? Maybe you'd rather roll. Whatever your rhythm, you must have picked up this book because you have some sort of interest in music. Scientifically speaking, you are not alone. Music is in our DNA. There is likely no human on the planet who has not been affected in some way by sound and vibration. Everyone experiences music. We use music to release and to rejoice, to learn and to mourn. We use music for wellness because music is one of humanity's oldest forms of spiritual medicine. Music, as we interpret and integrate it, involves principles of anthropology, biology, history, physiology, neuroscience, acoustics, aesthetics, and ethnomusicology.

Most individuals have some connection to and relationship with music. Whether it is intentional or not, we prescribe music for ourselves in nearly every aspect of our daily functioning. We have a workout playlist, a getting ready for work or school playlist, a cleaning playlist, a cooking playlist, a romance playlist, a goof-off playlist, a party playlist, a road trip playlist, a relaxation playlist.

We experience physical and emotional responses to music. A song can give you goosebumps, bring you to tears, get you moving, or conjure a memory. Music impacts us holistically—heart, soul, mind, and body—regardless of background or ability. Music is both a celebration and a mystery among all humankind.

Imagine consuming a movie, TV show, commercial, videogame—most any media—without music. The use of music can be very strategic. That wretched muzak in the elevator actually has a purpose! There are many functional uses of music in our everyday lives. One of the oldest uses of music is in ceremony—ritual, worship, civic, military, sports, etc. Music stimulates a specific response (to stand or pray), establishes ambiance, promotes a sense of belonging, focuses attention, arouses emotion, and can alter states of consciousness.

Another functional use of music is background music, which is played while the listener is primarily engaged in something else. You hear background music at a party, in the store, during dinner, or while creating. Background music breaks the monotony of repetitive tasks and can shift a mood. It might be used in the workplace to increase alertness after lunch or at the dentist's office to mask unpleasant sounds. Background music is often used to simply humanize an environment.

Entertainment and commercial uses of music are intended to create a mood, enhance emotions, maintain story continuity, induce memories, heighten the feeling of reality, and produce empathy. Work and industrial uses of music might involve a company chorus or band for social bonding and goodwill, which impacts productivity. Other functions of music include extra educational benefits (music can increase test scores, for example) and one of the oldest uses of music…healing.

If you believe music is therapeutic, you are in good company. Perhaps you use music to lift yourself up when you're feeling low or to sedate your overactive brain and body. Maybe you listen to the song that always takes you back to a specific event, which is so closely related to the song, you can remember a smell or what you were wearing. That memory accompanies you all day.

I can honestly say from personal and professional experience that music has the power and potential to positively affect and even change our lives. Whether it's for simple stress relief or for rewiring neurological pathways, music can be utilized in nearly all expanses of learning and healing. You may already be doing this in your activities of mundane normal life (however you define "normal").

Music has been a part of my life for as long as I can remember. One of my earliest memories is singing the old folk song *Love is Something if You Give it Away* at my maternal grandparents' fortieth wedding anniversary. I was four years old. My brothers and I were exposed to all types of live music performances, but my favorites were those in our own living room. I loved when company came for dinner because it meant gathering around the piano afterwards for a singalong (Mom's specialty). We regularly put on piano and singing recitals in that same living room. Even after my parents divorced, music was ever-present and encouraged.

My dad was a professional tenor and university professor of voice performance. He had a passion for all periods of classical music and opera, as well as Broadway, jazz, and folk. He conducted considerable research and published various pieces on British Art Song, a particularly dear genre. Oh, did I mention my family's claim to fame? When my dad sang with the Army Chorus, he performed for President Kennedy! Not too shabby.

My mom was a second grade through junior high music teacher nearly her entire career (she's a saint—or a sadist). When we were kids, she had a side gig playing piano and leading oldies singalongs at Granny's Closet restaurant/saloon in Tempe, Arizona. We got a kick out of seeing her perform and the enthusiastic response from the vociferous audience. Mom directed too many concerts and musicals to count, but some of the most memorable involved yours truly (I was one of my mom's students). I played Dorothy in *The Wizard of Oz* in the seventh grade and Laurie in

*Oklahoma* in the eighth grade. In case you're wondering, Mom recused herself from the auditions to avoid any accusations of favoritism (although my brothers still call BS). After retirement, Mom hasn't been able to sit still. She was the accompanist for many years of The Broadway Babies, who performed a new revue of Broadway songs and jazz standards annually in assisted living facilities. It provided for her an essential social and musical outlet.

My second mom, Mary, is an accomplished pianist, accompanist, and music pedagogian. She was another strong musical influence on me from the age of eleven. Shortly before that, my best friend, Meri, and I started making music together. Our musical connection began the day we met at JOT Camp, a summer day program through the Jewish Organization of Tempe, AZ. I was ten; Meri was eleven. A few years later, when we had graduated from campers to junior counselors, we formed our first band—a quad of dweeby teenagers (ages fourteen to sixteen), using pushed-together tables as a stage, with me as lead singer, a keyboardist, a guitar player, and a drummer, nailing Journey's *Don't Stop Believin'* (circa 1983).

Dad gave me my first real voice lesson in preparation for my role as Dorothy. I'll never forget him laying me down on the floor, on my back, to explain how to "breathe low." He had me breathe from my chest and then from my diaphragm, noting the visible difference in how the two areas of the body expand and contract. "Buddha belly" as opposed to "bursting boobies" (not that I had any yet) was and remains the preferred method for proper breath support.

Also in junior high, my choir attended a concert and workshop with Francine Reed, a local jazz gem you may recognize from her recordings with Lyle Lovett. At one point, Ms. Reed demonstrated the fabulous vocal jazz technique of scatting. She invited volunteers to the stage, and you might guess who the first to step up was. I channeled my inner Ella Fitzgerald and let it rip. I'll never forget Ms. Reed's response of, "Not bad for a white girl!" That was pretty sweet validation for a gawky thirteen-year-old! The experience was an absolute blast and authentic inspiration for this impressionable vocalist-in-training.

In addition to the school musicals, I sang in the advanced choir and played first chair flute up until high school. I then mostly left all of it behind because I became too cool for it. Except for choir. That was my tribe all through high school. I continued singing in choir when I studied broadcast journalism at Northern Arizona University. I sang backup for folk performers at local dives. Karaoke emerged right around my final year at NAU and that was a big source of expression, entertainment, and public drunkenness for many years to come. I sang in a local community choir for most of my twenties. My dad was the tenor soloist for one of our annual December Messiah performances, while I sang first soprano in the choir. I still have that recording on cassette tape. I toured and performed in London, Oxford, and Paris with part of that group in 1997.

Even though I hadn't pursued a degree or career in music initially, music and singing were always a prominent part of my existence and identity. I crashed bands in several states to jump on the mic or the percussion set. I performed at occasional weddings, gave voice lessons, and spent obscene amounts of money attending live music productions from 200-person audiences in the round to arena mayhem.

I have been singing and playing guitar, keyboard, and percussion with the same band o' knuckleheads for twenty-five years (with a few personnel changes, of course, but minimal drama). We have written and recorded some really groovy tunes. We have rocked backyard parties, corporate events, art festivals, chocolate festivals, animal rescue events, and weddings. We have spent more than twenty Labor Day weekends in the pines of northeastern Arizona for a musical camping commune of camaraderie, over-indulgence, and joyful noise. More on that band later, but its spirit has splintered off into various manifestations.

We were the studio musicians and producers for a mutual friend in 2005 to bring his original songs to fruition and professionally recorded a fantastic album fused with southern rock, folk, and gospel, titled *Skerlak Dead: A Waste of Oxygen*. I collaborated with another incredible group of eclectic musicians (most of us practicing board-certified music therapists) in 2011 to record an album of music written by our fearless leader, Stephanie Bianchi, titled *Synaptic Soul: Awake*. We performed our songs live at various events to spread a message of harmony through community, collective awareness, healing, and joy in the human condition. My partner and I frequently find ourselves entertaining and facilitating interactive music at dinner parties, campfires, and barbeques. We work cheap.

My music library comprises everything from Bach to Beck. Before music went digital, I had over a thousand CDs. I still cannot part with them, but haven't touched them in years. I still possess several LPs (one signed by all of Bon Jovi) and cassettes. I have a stack of 45s too. I suppose I keep all of it for nostalgia. Maybe it will be worth something someday, since the one hit wonder thing hasn't yet materialized.

These musical experiences and endeavors were a creative outlet for me as I spent ten years working in the media/PR industry. Some universal force began redirecting me as I hit a professional wall that coincided with my thirtieth birthday. I was attempting to meditate in a cave in the Grand Canyon's Havasupai Falls and had an epiphany. I needed more music in my life. I was dissatisfied in my profession and felt a pull toward music like I had never before experienced. I wanted music to be more than recreational for myself. I wanted to use music to connect with people beyond performance. I wanted to use music to help people.

I returned home and immediately jumped online to see what options Arizona State University offered for music careers. I didn't want to perform. I didn't want to focus on theory and composition. I didn't particularly want to teach, mostly because I like to eat and I don't do 7 a.m. meetings. Ever. I came across a description for ASU's music therapy program. I had never heard of it, but certainly believed that music has therapeutic value. I read on. I investigated further. I interviewed and shadowed a few local music therapists. I then scheduled a meeting with the incomparable Barbara J. Crowe, ASU's music therapy program director (now emeritus). When she further described the program and the profession to me, I knew in my guts that everything I had done previously had led me to this moment. I was going to be a music therapist.

I returned to peasant life and pursued an entirely different path and education. I earned a post-graduate Bachelor of Music degree in music therapy from ASU. After about five years of clinical practice, I was also teaching music therapy courses as a member of ASU's School of Music faculty. I was ready to deepen my practice and expand my teaching position, so while working beyond full-time, raising two young children, and managing a family, I earned a Master of Music degree in music therapy with a cognate in social gerontology and counseling, also from ASU.

I am a clinically trained, board-certified music therapist. I have worked with individuals from womb to tomb. The strategic use of music has positively influenced every single one of them. I employ music as the catalyst for therapeutic interaction to address psychosocial, cognitive, physical, communicative, and spiritual needs, helping individuals attain and maintain maximum levels of functioning. I have diverse, multicultural clinical experience with nearly all populations and settings, including medical/hospital, hospice, behavioral health, geriatrics, brain injury, developmental disabilities, and wellness. My clients and patients are everywhere from the Phoenix Zoo to Mayo Clinic.

I was a clinical professor for ASU's music therapy program for nine years, where I coordinated student placements for fieldwork and taught undergraduate and graduate courses in the areas of practicum, music competencies (voice, guitar, piano, and percussion), music therapy repertoire, children's music, psychology/neurology of music, basic counseling skills, improvisation, professional writing, and music therapy marketing. I have always enjoyed engaging in professional and community service with a creative, collaborative, and entrepreneurial spirit.

Enough resumé. Between my personal experiences with music and the near miracles I have witnessed as a practitioner of music, I have some mind-blowing stories. This book is essentially the musings of a music therapist, musician, music enthusiast, music consumer, music maker, and music facilitator. My stories, anecdotes, and nuggets of research reflect my experience as a clinician, an educator, and an everyday person. My musical identity is woven among each.

This is a collection of music and music therapy information, clinical vignettes, case studies, and abbreviated research. I believe anyone and everyone is the target audience of this content, so I chose not to write a textbook. My years in academia were incredibly fulfilling, but I am admittedly scarred by egos and politics. Plus, this content is meant for all. You will see pieces of my clinical research, but I keep it statistics-light. In other words, I do geek out now and then by throwing in some empirical tidbits and interesting facts, but I keep it to a minimum. Not required reading but rather, a memoir to share some of my stories—some of them inspiring, some heartbreaking, some hilarious. A celebration of a song's ability and potential, as well as an invitation and guide to consciously, deliberately, and therapeutically use music in your life. I hope you find it equally educational, entertaining, and useful.

Aaaand cue!

# II. EXPOSITION

*"Einstein, James Dean, Brooklyn's got a winning team, Davy Crockett, Peter Pan, Elvis Presley, Disneyland." —Billy Joel*

What exactly is music? At its simplest definition, music is a series of sounds and silences. My mentor, colleague, and friend, Barbara Crowe (2004) described "the phenomenon of music" as "an acoustic event involving specific combinations of sound moving over time."

Music is form, harmony, and expression. It is notes on a page, tempo, and dynamics, as instructed, articulated, and delivered. It is performed with various instruments and vocal techniques. It is an art form and a cultural activity. Music can be divided into multiple genres and sub-genres. We hear music live at concert and theater venues, and as an integral part of most media.

Music is one of the universal cultural aspects of all human society. It is a defining element of worship, ritual, and healing. Music is interchangeable with learning, history, and social identity. Consider how cohorts of abysmally treated individuals have bonded through the blues or spirituals. How folk music can bring fractured souls together to support and heal. How protest songs tell the ugly stories of unimaginable truths.

Music-effected benefits result from music's multiple functions. Crowe identified the following purposes of music: for pleasure/entertainment, aesthetic response (a response to "the beautiful" in art and nature), as a support to basic humanity, to touch the Divine, for communication, for its effects on activity level, and for support of human culture.

Music is both a process and a product. It is a function of nearly all aspects of everyday life, which we will examine further in later chapters. Let's first take a look at some basics.

A few definitions: *Pitch* refers to the high-low quality of a musical sound, determined by the frequency of its tone. *Rhythm* is a pattern of time, a recurring movement of sound, the relationship of tones over time (involves duration, beat, meter, tempo, and accent). *Melody* is a sequence of tones, a contoured movement of pitches and durations that form the main part of a piece of music. *Harmony* is the simultaneous occurrence of musical tones; it is the relationship of notes to each other, whether consonant (pleasant) or dissonant (tension-inducing). *Form* is the overall design of the music and how it progresses. Most world music traditions have culturally determined forms, including Western music with its sonatas and symphonies (overture, development, exposition, recapitulation, finale… wait a minute, this sounds familiar…) *Timbre* is also known as tone color—the unique character or quality of the sound as it relates to resonance and overtones. *Dynamics* is the variation in sound intensity or loudness—how quietly or loudly music is played or performed (pp or *pianissimo* is very soft; ff or *fortissimo* is very loud). Dynamics give music, particularly live music, its variety and personality.

I promised a painless history lesson, so let's explore the genres and artists. The following compilation is an extremely abbreviated history of music periods, popular genres, composers, and artists, reflecting significant events and innovations. This is by no means comprehensive and does not reflect any biases, although I can honestly say I have heard of every one of these composers/artists and I possess a majority in my music library.

Apologies if I inadvertently omitted any of your favorites. Write me and set me straight!

Countless synapses were firing (as were the wiki searches) in generating this list of music factoids. So much peripheral yet relevant information…the evolution of instruments…current events and politics in the chronology…recording and playback technology…pop culture…. Had to reign it in and narrow my focus.

We begin way back at the beginning of humankind and briefly review everything in between through 2020-ish. The last century is broken down by decade. Here, I use the term "artist" as an umbrella for composers and performers alike, in all genres of "popular music."

## Origins of Music

Many historians believe music existed before man existed and there are numerous theories about when and where music originated. Generally speaking, there are six identified periods of music in human history: Medieval Times/Middle Ages, Renaissance, Baroque, Classical, Romantic, and the Twentieth Century. Each period has a specific style and is a major contributor to what music is today.

## Medieval Times/Middle Ages, 500-1500 AD

Monophonic and Polyphonic were the two general types of musical styles.

- 590-604—The main forms of music included Gregorian Chant and Plainchant or Plainsong, a form of church music that involves only chanting or singing with no musical accompaniment.
- Around the fourteenth century, secular music became increasingly prominent.
- 850—The vocal structure of Gregorian Chant used in the Roman Catholic Church evolved from simple chants to parallel intervals,

which was the development of Polyphony and eventually Harmony.

- 1000-1100—The Troubadour and Trouvere developed traditions of secular song about chivalry and courtly love.
- 1150-1250—Rhythmic music notation appeared.

## Renaissance, 1400-1600 AD

The Church's control of the arts had weakened. Composers effected many changes in the way music was created and perceived by using instruments and creating more elaborate music forms for up to six voice parts. Modal characteristics of music evolved into Tonality with the increased use of fifths in root motion.

- 1584—A work titled, "A New Account of the Science of the Pitch-Pipes" by Chu Tsai-yu, was published in China, but would have a profound effect on Western music. Tsai-yu essentially solved the problem of equal temperament in that the natural seven octaves and the twelve perfect fifths equal temperament do not fit. They do not work mathematically or tonally. Tsai-yu determined that the fifths can be tempered not by relative lengths of the pipes, but by the ratios of their sizes. He calculated a formula that yielded a scale of evenly spaced notes where the semitones fit properly into the octave. What we call equal temperament today is a tuning system which approximates intervals by dividing an octave or other interval into twelve semitones of equal size. (Nerd alert!) The ratio of the frequencies of any adjacent pair of notes is the same, which is an equal perceived step size as the logarithm of frequency is perceived as pitch. This corrected the flaws in earlier tuning systems that were based on acoustically pure intervals—those which occur naturally in the overtone series.
- 1598—The first Italian Opera was produced, Jacopo Peri's *Dafne.*

### *Notable Composers of the Renaissance Period:*

- Gregorio Allegri
- William Byrd
- Pierre de La Rue
- Orlande de Lassus
- Claudio Monteverdi
- Jacopo Peri
- Giovanni Pierluigi da Palestrina
- Josquin Des Prez
- Thomas Tallis
- Tomas Luis de Victoria

## Baroque, 1600-1750

The Baroque Period is characterized by strict musical forms and highly ornamental works in Europe. The word "baroque" evolved from the Italian word "barocco," which means bizarre. During this period, composers experimented with form, musical contrasts, styles, and instruments with the development of instrumental music and opera. Music became homophonic, meaning a melody was supported by a harmony. Counterpoint and orchestral color made a stronger appearance. Prominent instruments in Baroque compositions featured violin, viola, double bass, harp, and oboe.

- 1620—Belgian mathematician Simon Stevin died. In his papers was the formula for equal temperament by Chu Tsai-yu from1584. Equal temperament was still an issue with the advancements in harmony and composition. It would still be many years before the issues were fully resolved; not until the era of Beethoven was the equally tempered scale fully adopted by Western composers.

- 1725—Antonio Vivaldi composed *The Four Seasons.*

### *Notable Composers of the Baroque Period:*

- Johan Sebastian Bach
- Arcangelo Corelli
- George Frideric Handel
- Claudio Monteverdi
- Johann Pachelbel
- Giovanni Battista Pergolesi
- Henry Purcell
- Jean-Philippe Rameau
- Antonio Salieri
- Alessandro Scarlatti
- Domenico Scarlatti
- Georg Philipp Telemann
- Antonio Vivaldi

## Classical, 1750-1830

Lighter and clearer than Baroque music, classical music is less complex and primarily homophonic. (Of course, if you prefer it and it ain't baroque, don't fix it. So. Very. Sorry.) The music styles of the classical period are characterized by simpler melodies and forms, such as sonatas. During this time, the middle class had more access to music when it was traditionally only available to nobility and aristocrats. To reflect this shift, composers wanted to create music that was less complicated and easier to understand. There was a rise in public taste for comic opera. The piano was the primary instrument of the period.

- 1742—Handel's *Messiah* premiered in Dublin, Ireland.

- 1775—The British soldiers stationed in America penned a simple tune to mock the Americans, titled *Yankee Doodle Dandy*. The Americans liked the catchy song and adopted it as their own.
- 1786—Mozart's *The Marriage of Figaro* opened in Vienna.
- 1789-1799 (The French Revolution)—Beethoven composed *Eroica*, his third symphony, which many believe marks the beginning of the romantic era. Beethoven also composed *Symphony No. 5*, considered by some as the most popular classical work ever written (dun dun dun duuunnnnn!).

### *Notable Composers of the Classical Period:*

- Carl Phillipp Emanuel Bach
- Ludwig van Beethoven
- Johannes Brahms
- Frederic Chopin
- Claude Debussy
- Christoph Willibald Gluck
- George Frideric Handel
- Franz Joseph Haydn
- Felix Mendelssohn
- Wolfgang Amadeus Mozart
- Maurice Ravel
- Giachino Rossini
- Chevalier de Saint-Georges
- Pyotr Ilyich Tchaikovsky
- Richard Wagner

## Romantic, 1830-1900

Music forms of the romantic period used music to tell a story or express an idea. Wind instruments enjoyed expanded use, particularly flute and saxophone. Melodies became fuller and more dramatic, as composers allowed their imaginations and intense emotions to soar through their works. By the mid-nineteenth century, folk music became popular and more emphasis was placed on nationalist themes.

- 1831—*America* (aka *My Country 'Tis of Thee*) was first performed.
- 1835—*Amazing Grace* was published to the tune of *New Britain* in William Walker's *The Southern Harmony*. This is the version most often sung today.
- 1835—The New York Philharmonic was founded (originally known as The Philharmonic Society of New York), now the oldest orchestra in America.
- 1845—*Leonora*, by William Henry Fry, was the first American Grand Opera.
- 1848—*Simple Gifts* was composed by Elder Joseph Brackett in Alfred, Maine, and later popularized in Aaron Copland's arrangement.
- 1861—Stephen Foster's biggest hit, *Old Folks at Home*, was published. He was known as the "Father of American Music" and a preeminent songwriter in nineteenth century America. His songs remain popular today...*Oh! Susanna*, *Camptown Races*, *Swannee River*, *Beautiful Dreamer*, and many others.
- 1855—*Auld Lang Syne* (aka *Song of the Old Folks*) was published.
- 1859—*Dixie* was written by Daniel Decatur Emmett in South Carolina.
- 1862—*The Battle Hymn of the Republic* was published.

- 1877—Thomas Edison invented the phonograph.
- 1881—Henry Lee Higginson formed the Boston Symphony Orchestra, which he ran for nearly forty years.
- 1883—The Metropolitan Opera opened in New York City.
- 1891—Carnegie Hall opened in New York City.
- 1893—*Happy Birthday* was composed by two teachers in Louisville, Kentucky.
- 1895—Spillers, the first record store, was founded in Cardiff, UK.
- 1895—Thomas Edison invented the motor-driven gramophone.
- 1897—Buddy Bolden organized the first band to play the instrumental blues (the forerunner of jazz) with repertoire including polkas, quadrilles, ragtime, and blues.
- 1899—While orchestral music remained popular, Scott Joplin ("The King of Ragtime") began to release a very new style of music including *Maple Time Rag*, which began the genre of ragtime, characterized by a syncopated, ragged rhythm.

### *Notable Composers of the Romantic Period:*

- Ludwig van Beethoven
- Hector Berlioz
- Georges Bizet
- Johannes Brahms
- Anton Bruckner
- Frederic Chopin
- Antonin Dvorak
- Gabriel Faure
- Stephen Foster
- Scott Joplin

- Franz Liszt
- Gustav Mahler
- Felix Mendelssohn
- Niccolo Paganini
- Giacomo Puccini
- Sergei Rachmaninoff
- Franz Schubert
- Clara Schumann
- Robert Schumann
- Jean Sibelius
- Johann Straus
- Johann Strauss II
- Pyotr Ilyich Tchaikovsky
- Giuseppe Verde
- Richard Wagner

## Twentieth Century

The music of the 1900s brought about many innovations. Artists were more willing to experiment with new music forms and used technology to enhance their compositions. Early electronic instruments included the dynamophone, Theremin, and Ondes-Martnot. Twentieth century music styles included impressionistic, twelve-tone system, neoclassical, jazz, concert music, musical theater, serialism, electronic music, new Romanticism, and minimalism. Popular music evolved, and then evolved some more, and more, and more.

- 1900-1960—Opera became increasingly popular.

- 1902—Victor and Columbia emerged as leaders in the phonograph field. The public started to buy phonographs and records (cylinders) for home use.
- 1903—Drawing from African traditions and spirituals, blues musicians were not yet well-known when musician W.C. Handy heard blues played in a train station. He publicized the genre and brought blues recordings to the public.
- 1904—While he never recorded, Buddy Bolden fused ragtime and blues, forming the basis of jazz.
- 1905—Columbia produced the first two-sided disc.
- 1907—The tango was introduced to America.
- Florenz Ziegfeld expanded the notion of Vaudeville stage shows to new heights by his elaborate productions known as *The Ziegfeld Follies.*
- 1908—*Take Me Out to the Ball Game* was the most popular song of the year.
- 1910—Jazz had become popular in New Orleans. A number of jazz genres later appeared throughout the country, with distinct regional variations.
- The fox trot dance craze began.
- In January, radio pioneer Lee De Forest experimented with radio by broadcasting two live performances from the stage of the New York Metropolitan Opera with an erratic signal that could be heard as far away as Newark, New Jersey. Music radio was born.
- 1912—*The Bird of Paradise* opened on Broadway in Daly's Theatre—the beginning of the Hawaiian music craze.
- 1914—A twelve-bar blues form based on the I-IV-V7 chord progression became standard.
- 1915—The Chicago Automatic Machine & Tool Company invented the jukebox.

- 1917—New Orleans jazz was a melting pot for blues, ragtime, and marching band styles.
- The cabaret business began in New York and eventually caused the shift of jazz from Chicago to New York.
- 1920—The first commercial American radio station, KDKA, began broadcasting.
- Country music, with its origins in the songs of the Appalachian Mountains, was developing into a popular new musical genre, particularly in the Southern states.
- 1922—In March, the Atlanta Journal opened up WSB in Atlanta, the first radio station in the south. Six months later, Fiddlin' John Carson made his radio debut as one of the first country music performers on the airwaves.
- 1923—Duke Ellington made his first recording on a cylinder, a stride piano piece, titled *Jig Walk*.
- Folk blues drew on the African experience, music, and spirituals, influencing later musical genres.
- 1927—The film *The Jazz Singer* was released in October, the first full length "Talkie"—motion picture with sound.
- Americans bought more than 100 million phonograph records.
- 1929—The 78 RPM record was introduced.
- 1930s—Jazz led to the birth of big band/swing music, a new genre of large bands playinglively dance music. Swing took on new meaning and was fully underway.
- 1931— On March 3, *The Star-Spangled Banner* was formalized as the National Anthem by a Congressional resolution, which was signed by President Herbert Hoover.
- The first network broadcast of the New York Metropolitan Opera was heard on December 25 with a performance of *Hänsel und Gretel*. The broadcast series came about in the early years of the

Great Depression to help the financially endangered Metropolitan Opera enlarge its audience and support through national exposure on network radio.

- 1933—Lonestar/Monogram film *Riders of Destiny*, starring a young John Wayne, was released, beginning the singing cowboy genre of films.
- Regular radio broadcasts of complete operas from the New York Metropolitan Opera began March 11, with the transmission of *Tristan und Isolde*.
- 1935—The big band era began, as well as the first recordings of gospel and blues.
- 1937—Woody Guthrie moved to Los Angeles and got a job at KFVD as a radio show host. He used the public platform to get his songs heard and tell stories of the Dust Bowl years in the American mid-west.
- 1938—The national boogie-woogie craze began.
- 1939—225,000 jukeboxes were in operation and responsible for the sale of 13 million records a year.
- 1940—Rhythm & blues (R&B) officially began, marketed primarily to African Americans, and characterized by a strong beat, with influences from more traditional blues.
- *Billboard Magazine* introduced the Hot 100 popularity chart in January. The week-by-week listings were based on statistics accrued by *Billboard Magazine* from record purchases and radio/jukebox play throughout the United States.
- South Carolina native Dizzy Gillespie began an innovative style of trumpet performance that would come to be called bebop.
- 1943—King Records, run by Syd Nathan, opened in Cincinnati to record hillbilly music. In 1946, they began recording R&B,

becoming one of the most prominent independent labels of the next decade.

- The Grand Ole Opry began airing nationally on more than 140 NBC affiliates.
- 1945—Though Capitol and Decca settled with the musician's union AFM by 1943, RCA, Victor, and Columbia held out for nearly two years more. The big bands never recovered, and the big band era was over.
- The Bihari family formed Modern Records in Los Angeles, one of the most successful and groundbreaking R&B labels in the country.
- Lew Chudd formed Imperial Records and the following year, Art Rupe formed Specialty Records, both in Los Angeles, to record R&B. Each label also made significant recordings of New Orleans R&B over the next decade and a half.
- 1946—*Choo Choo Ch'Boogie* by Louis Jordan & His Tympany Five became the biggest hit ever in the increasingly popular jump blues style that later led to rock 'n' roll.
- 1947—New York's Carnegie Hall welcomed Ernest Tubb and a group of Grand Ole Opry stars, acknowledging country music in the American musical lexicon.
- Ahmet Ertegun and Herb Abramson started Atlantic Records in September, which became the biggest R&B label in history.
- 1948—Columbia launched the vinyl 12-inch 33-1/3 RPM album in June.
- 1949—RCA Victor introduced the 45 RPM record, which was easier to produce, smaller, and cheaper than 78s. RCA Victor offered a small record player for $12.95 to play the new records.
- Multitrack magnetic recording began.

- 1950—Rock music combined various musical genres including blues, jazz, gospel, and country. It became largely guitar-driven and eventually fueled a growing youth culture.
- The Weavers' *Goodnight Irene* remained at the top of the charts for thirteen weeks and sold over a million copies. This was the first folk song to reach a broad audience and created a curiosity about folk and Americana music.
- The R&B ballad and doo-wop took shape.
- 1951—The first jukebox to play 45 RPM records was introduced.
- A wave of young black vocal groups emerged with variations of the style popularized by the Orioles.
- In July, Cleveland disc jockey Alan Freed began his Moondog Show on WJW, broadcasting nothing but R&B. He coined the phrase "rock 'n' roll" to describe the music.
- 1952—In New Orleans, the rock 'n' roll beat was furthered by Lloyd Price's hit *Lawdy Miss Clawdy* with Fats Domino on piano.
- 1953—Fifteen million R&B records were purchased. While that only accounted for 5% of all records sold, it drew attention in the industry.
- Soul music emerged.
- The R&B charts began to reflect the overwhelming dominance of emerging rock 'n' roll.
- In June, the first major integrated rock 'n' roll show was staged in Cleveland with headlining co-stars The Dominoes and Bill Haley & His Comets.
- The Radio Industry Association of America (RIAA) arrived at a standard equalization curve for the recording and playback of records, clearing the way to manufacture standardized preamplifiers and better sounding playback equipment such as speakers, amplifiers, phonograph cartridges, and turntables.

- In August, eighteen-year-old Elvis Aaron Presley wandered into the street-front office of Sun Records in Memphis and approached receptionist Marion Keisker, asking to pay for a demo recording as a gift for his mother.
- 1954—R&B music exploded into the mainstream with black vocal groups leading the crossover.
- Pop record companies tried desperately to capitalize on the fad by having white artists cover black vocal group records. The increased distribution and radio play assured many of those versions of becoming hits.
- In July, Elvis returned to Sun Records in Memphis at the request of owner Sam Phillips. Phillips had assembled guitarist Winfield "Scotty" Moore and upright bass player Bill Black to see if he could capture something the public might like with the talented young singer. Rockabilly was born.
- 10,000 fans attended Alan Freed's first east coast Rock 'n' Roll Show held in Newark, New Jersey, featuring the Clovers and the Harptones. The success was further indication that rock 'n' roll had national appeal.
- Freed moved to New York's WINS in September and quickly became the city's most famous DJ, attracting large audiences to his newly named Rock 'n' Roll Party.
- 1955—After being used in the hit film about juvenile delinquency, *Blackboard Jungle*, Bill Haley & His Comets' *Rock Around the Clock* became the first rock 'n' roll record to top the Pop Charts, holding the number one position for two months and remaining in the Top 100 for a record thirty-eight weeks. It would be thirty-nine years before that record was broken.
- In May, the first rock 'n' roll long-playing record (LP) was released by Bill Haley & His Comets. Higher priced full-length

albums limited their appeal for teenagers and remained largely the realm of adult pop singers for another decade.

- With censorship prevalent, white cover records still held a slight edge in radio play but not in sales.
- Rock 'n' roll music received a mention in the year-end Encyclopedia Britannica music review, which derogatorily referred to it in racist terms as "jungle music."
- 1956—Elvis scored five number one hits in a seven-month span and caused a sensation with his performance of *Hound Dog* on *The Milton Berle Show*. He appeared twice on *The Ed Sullivan Show* in the fall to big ratings, and released his first film that November.
- Rock 'n' roll entered the movies with cheaply made exploitation films featuring cameos by artists singing their latest hits.
- 1957—The first test of FM broadcasting was performed by NHK in Japan.
- On his final *Ed Sullivan* appearance, Elvis was filmed from the waist up. The screams from the studio audience only made what the home viewer was missing more suggestive.
- *Jailhouse Rock*, starring Elvis, introduced a precursor to the rock video, as the title song had an elaborate setting in a jail cell and was choreographed by Elvis himself.
- Bill Haley & His Comets toured Europe, setting off riots and bringing rock 'n' roll to the continent for the first time.
- An Australian tour featuring Jerry Lee Lewis and Buddy Holly made rock 'n' roll a worldwide phenomenon. Lewis' performance of *Whole Lotta Shakin' Goin' On* that July on *The Steve Allen Show* brought rock 'n' roll music more reprimands after Lewis kicked over his piano stool and played the keyboards with disturbing

wild-eyed intensity. The ratings, however, beat the top-ranked *Ed Sullivan Show* for the first time that year.

- The stroll became the first dance associated with rock 'n' roll.
- In a move to tame rock 'n' roll, ABC television launched the national version of a Philadelphia program called *American Bandstand*, which promoted the more wholesome side of rock 'n' roll.
- Atlantic Records began to record and release stereo records.
- 1958—In June, Jerry Lee Lewis' first English tour resulted in scandal when it was learned that his third wife was his thirteen-year-old second cousin. He cut the tour short and was blackballed by American radio and television.
- *Billboard Magazine* began the Hot 100, expanding the pop charts to allow more records to become certified hits.
- The EIA and RIAA established the 45/45 system for recording and reproducing stereo phonograph records.
- 1959—Buddy Holly, Ritchie Valens, and J.P. Richardson (The Big Bopper) died in a plane crash while on tour in Clearlake, Iowa, on February 3. It became known as "The Day the Music Died" and was memorialized in Don McLean's 1972 hit, *American Pie.* All three were at the peak of their popularity and had collectively, in twelve months, sold over ten million records worldwide.
- Congress opened the payola hearings designed to squash rock 'n' roll DJs who received money from record distributors in exchange for airplay, a common practice in all forms of radio for years. Alan Freed was its main target and became its biggest casualty, after he was found guilty and taken off the air.
- Radio stations responded by voluntarily putting severe restrictions on what they would play, including widely adopting the

Top 40 format, which limited how many songs were approved for airing.

- Dick Clark acted quickly to distance himself from rock 'n' roll's negative image as he increasingly showcased teen idols on *American Bandstand.*
- The first Grammy Award was presented by the National Academy of Recording Arts and Sciences (originally titled the Gramophone Awards). The song of the year was awarded to Domenico Modugno for *Nel Blu Dipinto Di Blu (Volare).*
- The rock instrumental had its biggest year ever in response to rock music facing bans for lyrical content.
- Bossa nova was born—a style of Brazilian music fusing samba and jazz, developed and popularized in Brazil during the 1950s and 1960s.
- The Newport Folk Festival was founded by Theodore Bikel, Oscar Brand, Pete Seeger, George Wein (founder of the Newport Jazz Festival), and his partner Albert Grossman. The concept was to elevate the music of the people to greater public prominence.
- Berry Gordy started Tamla-Motown Records, which eventually became the most successful black-owned and operated company in American history (not just in music) with 600 million records sold.
- Since 1955, the market share for rock 'n' roll had increased from 15.7% to 42.7%, making it the fastest-growing style of music ever.
- 1960—Contemporary folk revived folk music, integrating musical traditions from around the world.
- In September, the FCC banned payola.
- 1961—The FCC adopted the Zenith/GE system standard for FM broadcasting.
- FM broadcasts began in the United States.

- 1962—The Beatles released *Love Me Do*, which peaked on the UK charts at number seventeen. It would reach the top of the US singles charts in May of 1964.
- 1963—The first compact cassette recorder was released by Phillips.
- The Beatles' second album, *With the Beatles*, was released on November 22—the same day John F. Kennedy was shot. By the end of the first week of release, the album had sold more than 500,000 copies. *I Want to Hold Your Hand* was released as a single near the end of the year and reached the top of both the American and British charts. The path was clear for the Beatles to launch an American tour.
- The Twist craze was diminishing and record companies began to shift toward the surf music boom.
- Odetta performed the song *I'm On My Way* in front of the Lincoln Memorial, with Reverend Martin Luther King Jr. right behind her during the March on Washington. The song became an anthem for the Civil Rights Movement.
- 1964—On February 1, The Beatles' *I Want to Hold Your Hand* went to number one on the U.S. Billboard Chart. It held that position for seven weeks. The single sold a million copies in the first two weeks.
- On February 9, the Beatles made their first live American television appearance on *The Ed Sullivan Show*. Approximately 74 million viewers—almost half the American population—watched the performance.
- 1965—The first eight-track tape player became available for commercial use.
- 1966—A new TV situation comedy was aired to appeal to the growing Baby Boom market of teenagers; *The Monkees* debuted

on NBC. The group was manufactured by producers at NBC and fed carefully crafted hit songs that were heavily promoted on radio and the new music medium, television.

- The success of *The Monkees* forced a young English singer to change his name from David Jones to David Bowie.
- 1967—The Monterey International Pop Festival was held June 16-18 on the Monterey County Fairgrounds in Monterey, California. This was the first widely promoted festival of rock music and regarded as the beginning of the Summer of Love. The promoters, Lou Adler, John Phillips (of The Mamas & the Papas), Alan Pariser, and Derek Taylor wanted rock to be elevated artistically to the prominence of folk and jazz. The festival helped place California at the center of the music counterculture and became a template for future rock festivals.
- Clive Davis became president of Columbia Records. He began to sign folk-rock and rock bands to Columbia. He viewed the new sound as the future of popular music. Columbia doubled its market share within three years.
- June 25 saw the first international satellite television broadcast with the Beatles performing *All You Need Is Love* on the show *Our World*. The estimated viewing audience was 400 million.
- The first audio cassette player (mono) designed for use in car dashboards was introduced.
- 1969—The Woodstock Music & Arts Fair, billed as "An Aquarian Exposition: Three Days of Peace and Music," was held at a 600-acre farm owned by Max Yasgur in White Lake, New York, August 15-18. The gathering was estimated at 500,000.
- A free concert at the Altamont Speedway in Northern California was organized on December 6 by The Grateful Dead, The Rolling Stones, and others to be a "Woodstock West." The event drew approximately 300,000 people. The Altamont Speedway Free

Festival suffered considerable violence, including one homicide and three accidental deaths. The crowds were not peaceful. Drug use and lack of facilities contributed to the unrest. Ironically, the Grateful Dead never played due to the level of violence. There were four births on-site during the day of the festival, however.

- Buck Owens brought his Bakersfield Honky Tonk style of playing to the broader American public with regular appearances on the new TV show *Hee Haw*. Roy Clark brought the five-string banjo back to popularity at the same venue.
- 1970—Rap and hip-hop established their origins in 1970s New York City house parties. These genres initially relied upon the beats found in funk, soul, and disco, but provided a new form of expression.
- James Taylor released *Fire and Rain* and emerged as an individual voice, a singer-songwriter with a personal perspective and something to say. The singer-songwriter era began.
- On February 26, National Public Radio replaced the National Educational Radio Network, following congressional passage of the Public Broadcasting Act of 1967.
- 1971—August 1 saw the birth of large-scale benefit concerts. The Concert for Bangladesh (relief for the 1970 Bhola cyclone) was organized by George Harrison. The concert attracted more than 40,000 people for two shows at New York City's Madison Square Garden.
- 1973—Ampex developed the A standard for One Inch Video Tape Recording (VTR).
- Clive Davis was fired from Columbia for using company funds to pay for his son's Bar Mitzvah. The larger political issues for Columbia were the allegations of corporate payola for DJs to saturate airplay of Davis' Columbia artists.

- After writing his memoirs, Clive Davis became the president of Arista records. He continued his long history of recognizing and signing major talents to the new label.
- 1974—Rebellious punk rock developed with limited instrumentation, harsh sound, and shorter songs. Lyrics were typically anti-establishment.
- 1975—Betamax video cassette tape recording format was released by Sony for television and quality sound recordings.
- 1976—VHS videocassette tape recording format was released by JVC.
- 1977—The film *Saturday Night Fever* sparked a new lifestyle, disco.
- 1978—LaserDisc technology was released and marketed as Discovervision. It was the first optical format and the precursor to the CD and DVD.
- 1979 —Sony introduced a portable music listening device in July, the Walkman. The small cassette player could be carried in a pocket and used with small headphones. A new market was established.
- 1980—John Lennon was fatally shot at the age of 40 on December 8 in the archway of The Dakota in New York, New York.
- 1981—Phillips and Sony joined forces to establish a standard for compact disc recording, Phillips DAC1. The CD was born.
- Music Television (MTV) was launched on August 1 by a New York City-based cable network to play music videos hosted by on-air hosts who became known as Video Jockeys (VJs).
- 1982—The CD was launched in Japan in October.
- Musical Instrument Digital Interface (MIDI) was defined as an industry-standard protocol enabling electronic musical instruments (including keyboards) to communicate with computers.

A MIDI trigger could generate any sound sample or waveform within a computer program that could then be directed to an amplifier and speakers.

- Michael Jackson released the album *Thriller*, which quickly became the highest selling album in history, topping 25 million sold.
- 1983—January 1 is considered the birthday of the internet.
- The CD was launched worldwide in March.
- *The Dark Side of the Moon* by Pink Floyd became the longest-running album ever on the Billboard charts at 491 weeks.
- 1984—The first Video Music Awards were held at Radio City Music Hall in New York, created by the relatively new MTV. The event was hosted by Bette Midler and Dan Aykroyd. The awards were statuettes of an astronaut on the moon with an American flag. Awards were given to Michael Jackson, Cyndi Lauper, the Police, and Herbie Hancock.
- 1985—Madonna launched her first major tour, The Virgin Tour.
- 1986—The Beastie Boys debuted *License to Kill*, the first rap album to reach number one.
- 1987—Digital Audio Tape (DAT) was released by Sony as a recording and playback system, which made it possible to make an exact copy of CDs or any other audio source (16-bit, 48, 44.1 or 32 kHz sampling rates). This made the CD industry nervous.
- 1988—Vinyl records were outsold by CDs.
- 1989—MTV launched *Unplugged* and brought fresh performances of major and minor acts to the acoustic world, breathing new life into classic music and its heroes.
- 1991—MP3 was developed as a digital audio recording format, highly compressed for low memory storage, and approved as an ISO/IEC standard. There was now a standard format for music

compression that could allow music to be sent easily over the internet.

- Grunge went mainstream with the release of Nirvana's *Smells Like Teen Spirit.*
- 1993—On April 30, the internet became available to the public and began to flourish.
- 1994—Dave Matthews and the Dave Matthews Band reached public consciousness as an acoustic jam band.
- 1995—The Rock and Roll Hall of Fame grand opening was held in Cleveland on September 2. The ribbon was cut by a small group that included Yoko Ono and Little Richard.
- 1996—The DVD was introduced.
- Tupac Shakur was killed at the age of 25 in a drive-by shooting on September 7 in Las Vegas, Nevada.
- 1997—Sarah McLachlan, frustrated that the music industry assumed it was not good business practice to book two women acts in the same line-up, started the Lilith Fair Festival with an all-female line-up. It was the top-grossing tour of the year.
- 1999—Nineteen-year-old Shawn Fanning, a Northeastern University freshman, created Napster. By writing code, he pioneered peer-to-peer file sharing, removed the big music studios and major retailers as profit-minded intermediaries, and created an entirely new paradigm for music and media consumption.
- 2001—iTunes was introduced by Apple as a proprietary digital media player application to organize, distribute, and maintain some copyright control over audio and video media. Songs could be found, purchased, and catalogued individually.
- On October 23, iPod portable media players were introduced by Apple to store and play music and videos purchased on iTunes.

- XM Satellite Radio was launched on September 25 as a digital radio service with seventy-three music channels, thirty-nine news, talk, sports, and entertainment channels, twenty-three play-by-play sports channels, and twenty-one regional traffic and weather channels. The new service was subscription-based at $9.95 per month, per receiver.
- Napster was attacked with traditional lawsuits and forced to shut down for encouraging, aiding, and abetting copyright infringement.
- 2002—Sirius Satellite Radio was launched nationwide as competition to XM Satellite Radio on July 1.
- 2003—On April 28, Apple unveiled the iTunes Music Store, where music could be downloaded for 99 cents per song. It was a theoretical win-win with small amounts of money, legal rights, and artists being paid. It was not at all clear whether the system would work since it was so easy to download music for free. The landscape of music distribution was changing now that consumers could legally buy the music they wanted, as opposed to buying entire albums for a single song. Every track had to compete for the public's acceptance.
- 2005—YouTube was introduced in April.
- Pandora was introduced in September.
- 2007—SoundCloud was launched in August.
- Amazon Prime Music launched in September.
- 2008—During the George W. Bush administration, the FCC approved the merger of the only two competing satellite radio providers, XM Satellite Radio and Sirius Satellite Radio. On July 29, the merger was complete and a monopoly was established in satellite, subscription-based, radio distribution.
- Spotify was introduced in October.

- 2010—iPod sales rose to 52.3 million units from only 381,000 in the year 2000. Video game industry sales topped $19.6 billion, up from $6.6 billion in 2000.
- 2011—Digital sales of individual music tracks exceeded CD sales for the first time; 300 million CDs were sold.
- 2015—Lin Manuel Miranda's musical about Alexander Hamilton premiered on January 20.
- Apple Music was launched in June.
- 2017—Streaming because the revenue leader of the American music industry.
- 2019—TikTok established itself in the media industry as more than a fad.
- 2020—Billie Eilish made Grammy history at the age of 18 when she took home the top four prizes: best new artist, record of the year, album of the year, and song of the year.
- COVID-19 hit the music world. Virtual performances and balcony concerts kept people socially connected through music.

(Liveaboutmusic, 2021; Softschools, 2021; The People History, 2021, Wikipedia, 2021; Wyeth, 2018)

### *Notable Classical, Broadway, and Early Popular Music Composers of the 20th Century:*

- Samuel Barber
- Irving Berlin
- Leonard Bernstein
- Benjamin Britten
- John Cage
- Elliott Carter
- Aaron Copland

- Fred Ebb
- Danny Elfman
- Dorothy Fields
- George Gershwin
- Ira Gershwin
- Marvin Hamlisch
- Woodie Guthrie
- Oscar Hammerstein II
- Marvin Hamlisch
- Lorenz Hart
- Charles Ives
- Scott Joplin
- John Kander
- Jerome Kern
- Zoltan Kodaly
- Jonathan Larson
- Alan Jay Lerner
- Frank Loesser
- Frederick Loewe
- Alan Menken
- Carl Orff
- Cole Porter
- Sergey Prokofiev
- Maurice Ravel
- Tim Rice
- Richard Rodgers
- Eric Satie

- Arnold Schoenberg
- Aleksandr Scriabin
- Pete Seeger
- Richard Sherman
- Robert Sherman
- Dmitry Shostakovich
- Stephen Sondheim
- John Phillip Sousa
- Igor Stravinsky
- Andrew Lloyd Webber
- Kurt Weill
- Ralph Vaughan Williams
- John Williams
- Meredith Willson

Look at America's progression of "Popular Music" and its influences before we break it down further.

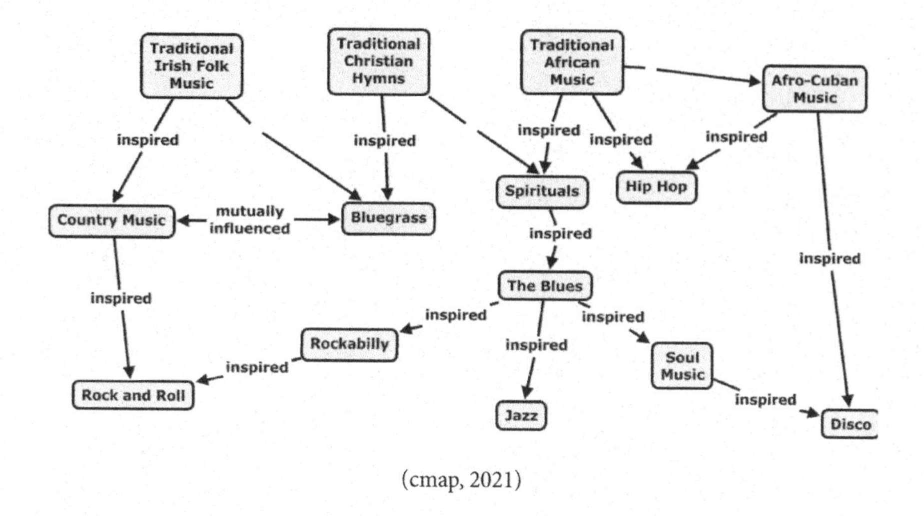


(cmap, 2021)

## Popular Twentieth Century-Plus Music by Decade

1920s—The decade was dominated by jazz, blues, big band, traveling dance bands, ragtime, and boogie-woogie. Following the devastation of WWI, 1920s music was upbeat and optimistic as the economy boomed and the parties "roared," despite prohibition. The music industry was just beginning.

### *Popular 1920s Artists:*

- Louis Armstrong
- Eddie Cantor
- Duke Ellington
- Ma Rainey
- Bessie Smith
- Sophie Tucker
- Paul Whiteman

1930s—The Great Depression heavily influenced the music of the time. Blues, country, and gospel reflected the hardships faced by many, while optimism was maintained by big band and swing.

### *Popular 1930s Artists:*

- Roy Acuff
- The Andrews Sisters
- Fred Astaire
- Gene Autry
- Cab Calloway
- Count Basie
- Bing Crosby
- Tommy Dorsey
- Benny Goodman
- Mahalia Jackson
- Robert Johnson

1940s—The decade mirrored the pain of WWII while looking toward a positive future. Many artists entertained troops through the United States Service Organization (USO). Music consisted of jazz, big band, swing, Broadway, country, bebop, novelty acts, and band leaders.

### *Popular 1940s Artists:*

- Roy Acuff
- The Andrews Sisters
- Count Basie
- Dave Brubek
- Maria Callas
- Rosemary Clooney

- Nat King Cole
- Bing Crosby
- Miles Davis
- Dorsey Brothers
- Ella Fitzgerald
- Judy Garland
- Stan Getz
- Dizzy Gillespie
- Billie Holiday
- John Lee Hooker
- Gene Kelly
- Peggy Lee
- Mary Martin
- Ethel Merman
- Glenn Miller
- Thelonious Monk
- The Orioles
- Charlie Parker
- Oscar Peterson
- Artie Shaw
- Elizabeth Schwarzkopf
- Renata Tebaldi
- T-Bone Walker

1950s—The decade represented a simple, wholesome time, as well as the beginnings of major social changes. Radio and television exposed the nation to a greater variety of artists and styles. Some of the first music superstars emerged, dominating the airwaves and the fantasies of young girls. Popular genres included rock 'n' roll, R&B, Motown, traditional pop, country, jazz, blues, calypso, and vocal jazz.

### *Popular 1950s Artists:*

- Julie Andrews
- Eddy Arnold
- Gene Autry
- Chet Baker
- Harry Belafonte
- Tony Bennett
- Chuck Berry
- Pat Boone
- Teresa Brewer
- Ruth Brown
- Dave Brubek
- Maria Callas
- Glen Campbell
- Johnny Cash
- June Carter Cash
- The Chantels
- Ray Charles
- Patsy Cline
- The Coasters
- Nat King Cole

- John Coltrane
- Sam Cooke
- Sammy Davis Jr.
- Miles Davis
- Doris Day
- Bo Diddley
- The Drifters
- The Everly Brothers
- Fats Domino
- Ella Fitzgerald
- Stan Getz
- Dizzy Gillespie
- Buddy Holly
- John Lee Hooker
- Lena Horne
- Shirley Jones
- Gene Kelly
- BB King
- Mario Lanza
- Peggy Lee
- Jerry Lee Lewis
- Little Richard
- Julie London
- Frankie Lymon & the Teenagers
- Dean Martin
- Mary Martin
- Carmen McRae

- Ethel Merman
- Charles Mingus
- The Miracles
- Thelonious Monk
- Bill Monroe
- Ricky Nelson
- The Orioles
- Patti Page
- Charlie Parker
- Oscar Peterson
- The Platters
- Elvis Presley
- J.P. Richardson ("The Big Bopper")
- Chita Rivera
- Marty Robbins
- Elizabeth Schwartzkopf
- The Shirelles
- Frank Sinatra
- Renata Tebaldi
- The Temptations
- Mel Tillis
- Conway Twitty
- Ritchie Valens
- Sarah Vaughan
- T-Bone Walker
- Muddy Waters
- Andy Williams

- Hank Williams
- Jackie Wilson

1960s—Music was becoming a dichotomy of ultimate commercialism with manufactured bands (The Monkees, The Archies, etc.) and revolutionary artists with some of the singer-songwriter and instrumentalist GOATS emerging on the scene (Bob Dylan, Jimi Hendrix, etc.). The British Invasion characterized much of the decade. Popular genres included folk, surf rock, psychedelic rock, blues, Motown, progressive rock, pop, soul, R&B, country, British Invasion, Latin rock, and protest music.

### *Popular 1960s Artists:*

- Julie Andrews
- Eddy Arnold
- Burt Bacharach
- Joan Baez
- Chet Baker
- The Band
- The Beach Boys
- The Beatles
- Chuck Berry
- Booker T. & The MGs
- James Brown
- Ruth Brown
- Dave Brubek
- Buffalo Springfield
- The Byrds
- Maria Callas
- Glenn Campbell

- The Carpenters
- Carol Channing
- The Chantels
- Ray Charles
- Chubby Checker
- Patsy Cline
- The Coasters
- Nat King Cole
- John Coltrane
- Chick Corea
- Cream
- Creedence Clearwater Revival
- Neil Diamond
- Bo Diddley
- Placido Domingo
- The Doors
- The Drifters
- Bob Dylan
- Ella Fitzgerald
- The Four Tops
- Aretha Franklin
- Marvin Gaye
- Stan Getz
- Dizzy Gillespie
- Leslie Gore
- The Grateful Dead
- Joel Grey

- Arlo Guthrie
- Woody Guthrie
- Buddy Guy
- Merle Haggard
- Jimi Hendrix
- John Lee Hooker
- Lena Horne
- Etta James
- Jefferson Airplane
- Waylon Jennings
- Shirley Jones
- Tom Jones
- Janis Joplin
- Madeline Kahn
- BB King
- Ben E. King
- The Kinks
- Gladys Knight & The Pips
- Angela Lansbury
- Led Zeppelin
- Jerry Lee Lewis
- Loretta Lynn
- The Mamas & The Papas
- Henry Mancini
- Martha & The Vandellas
- Mary Martin
- Liza Minelli

- Charles Mingus
- The Miracles
- Thelonious Monk
- The Moody Blues
- Rita Moreno
- Van Morrison
- Zero Mostel
- Ricky Nelson
- Willie Nelson
- Jerry Orbach
- Roy Orbison
- Dolly Parton
- Luciano Pavorotti
- Bernadette Peters
- Oscar Peterson
- The Platters
- Charley Pride
- Otis Redding
- The Righteous Brothers
- Chita Rivera
- Marty Robbins
- Smoky Robinson & The Miracles
- The Rolling Stones
- Elizabeth Schwartzkopf
- Neil Sedaka
- The Shirelles
- Simon & Garfunkel

- Percy Sledge
- Sonny & Cher
- Dusty Springfield
- The Stanley Brothers
- The Statler Brothers
- Steppenwolf
- Barbra Streisand
- The Supremes
- Renata Tebaldi
- The Temptations
- Mel Tillis
- Three Dog Night
- Ike & Tina Turner
- Conway Twitty
- Franki Valli &The Four Seasons
- Sarah Vaughan
- The Velvet Underground
- T-Bone Walker
- Andy Williams
- Hank Williams, Jr.
- Jackie Wilson
- Stevie Wonder
- Tammy Wynette

1970s—Disco became one of the biggest and most despised music trends of the decade. Disco was so pervasive that many established singers and bands released disco songs to keep current (Blondie, Rod Stewart, etc.). Heavier rock music and punk rock surfaced, partly in retaliation for disco. Popular genres included disco/dance, progressive rock, punk, new wave, funk, soul, glam rock, soft rock, singer-songwriter, folk, southern rock, country, country pop, and power pop.

### *Popular 1970s Artists:*

- ABBA
- AC/DC
- Aerosmith
- The Allman Brothers
- America
- Asleep at the Wheel
- Bachman Turner Overdrive
- Bad Company
- Joan Baez
- Chet Baker
- The Band
- The Beach Boys
- Beastie Boys
- The Bee Gees
- Black Sabbath
- Blondie
- Boston
- David Bowie
- Jackson Browne

- Dave Brubek
- Jimmy Buffett
- Glenn Campbell
- The Carpenters
- The Cars
- Carol Channing
- Harry Chapin
- Cheap Trick
- Chicago
- The Chi-Lites
- Eric Clapton
- The Clash
- Joe Cocker
- Leonard Cohen
- John Coltrane
- The Commodores
- Alice Cooper
- Chick Corea
- Michael Crawford
- Creedence Clearwater Revival
- Jim Croce
- Crosby Stills Nash & Young
- Deep Purple
- John Denver
- Neil Diamond
- Dire Straits
- Placido Domingo

- The Doobie Brothers
- The Doors
- Bob Dylan
- The Eagles
- Earth Wind & Fire
- Electric Light Orchestra
- Emerson Lake & Palmer
- Fleetwood Mac
- Foreigner
- The Four Tops
- Peter Frampton
- Aretha Franklin
- Marvin Gaye
- Crystal Gayle
- Stan Getz
- Gloria Gaynor
- Grand Funk Railroad
- The Grateful Dead
- Joel Grey
- Arlo Guthrie
- Woody Guthrie
- Merle Haggard
- Emmylou Harris
- George Harrison
- Heart
- Iggy Pop
- The Isley Brothers

- The Jackson Five
- Waylon Jennings
- Jethro Tull
- Elton John
- Billy Joel
- Shirley Jones
- Tom Jones
- Janis Joplin
- Journey
- Chaka Kahn
- Madeline Kahn
- Kansas
- Carole King
- The Kinks
- KISS
- Kool & The Gang
- Kris Kristofferson
- Angela Lansbury
- Led Zeppelin
- John Lennon
- Gordon Lightfoot
- Kenny Loggins
- Patti LuPone
- Loretta Lynn
- Lynyrd Skynyrd
- Henry Mancini
- Barry Manilow

- Bob Marley
- Curtis Mayfield
- Paul McCartney
- Reba McEntire
- Alan Menken
- Bette Midler
- The Steve Miller Band
- Ronnie Milsap
- Charles Mingus
- Liza Minelli
- Joni Mitchell
- The Moody Blues
- Rita Morena
- Van Morrison
- Zero Mostel
- Anne Murray
- Willie Nelson
- Olivia Newton-John
- Nitty Gritty Dirt Band
- Jessye Norman
- Ted Nugent
- The O'Jays
- Jerry Orbach
- Parliament
- Alan Parsons
- Dolly Parton
- Luciano Pavorotti

- Bernadette Peters
- Oscar Peterson
- Tom Petty
- Pink Floyd
- The Pointer Sisters
- Charley Pride
- John Prine
- Queen
- The Ramones
- Lou Reed
- Chita Rivera
- Marty Robbins
- Kenny Rogers
- The Rolling Stones
- Linda Ronstadt
- Diana Ross
- Rufus
- Rush
- Otis Rush
- Santana
- Bob Seger
- The Sex Pistols
- Sly & The Family Stone
- Carly Simon
- Paul Simon
- Patti Smith
- Bruce Springsteen

- Stanley Brothers
- The Staple Singers
- Steely Dan
- Rod Stewart
- Cat Stevens (Yusaf)
- Styx
- The Sugarhill Gang
- Donna Summer
- Supertramp
- James Taylor
- Renata Tebaldi
- Thin Lizzy
- Three Dog Night
- Mell Tillis
- The Marshall Tucker Band
- Tanya Tucker
- Conway Twitty
- Van Halen
- Stevie Ray Vaughan
- The Velvet Underground
- Ben Vereen
- War
- Barry White
- The Who
- Colm Wilkinson
- Andy Williams
- Hank Williams Jr.

- Bill Withers
- Stevie Wonder
- Tammy Wynette
- Yes
- ZZ Top

1980s—MTV dramatically changed music during the decade of excess. Videos became a necessity for artists to gain popularity and sell records. A greater importance was placed on the appearance of musicians and gimmicks became commonplace. Michael Jackson was one of the dominant artists of the decade, partly due to his creative music videos setting new pop music standards. New wave and electronic music paired nicely with the beginnings of the computer age. Hair bands also became popular with their theatrical and outrageous videos and performances. Hip-hop came into the mainstream. Genres included new wave, synth-pop, hair metal, hip-hop, gothic rock, heavy metal, pop, alternative rock, hardcore punk, contemporary R&B, and country.

*Popular 1980s Artists:*

- 38 Special
- Paula Abdul
- AC/DC
- Bryan Adams
- Aerosmith
- Alabama
- Asleep at the Wheel
- The B-52s
- Chet Baker
- The Bangles

- Kathleen Battle
- Pat Benatar
- Berlin
- Blondie
- Andrea Bocelli
- Bon Jovi
- David Bowie
- Beastie Boys
- Sarah Brightman
- Garth Brooks
- Bobby Brown
- Jackson Browne
- Dave Brubek
- Betty Buckley
- Kate Bush
- Glenn Campbell
- Jose Carreras
- The Cars
- Tracy Chapman
- Cheap Trick
- Cher
- Chicago
- Eric Clapton
- The Clash
- Leonard Cohen
- Phil Collins
- Chick Corea

- Elvis Costello
- Michael Crawford
- Culture Club
- Def Leppard
- Depeche Mode
- Devo
- Neil Diamond
- Diamond Rio
- Dire Straits
- Placido Domingo
- Duran Duran
- Sheena Easton
- Enya
- Gloria Estefan
- Eurhythmics
- Harvey Fierstein
- Fleetwood Mac
- Renee Fleming
- Foreigner
- Peter Gabriel
- Crystal Gayle
- Genesis
- Vince Gill
- The Go-Gos
- Lee Greenwood
- Guns 'N Roses
- Merle Haggard

- Hall & Oates
- Herbie Hancock
- Emmylou Harris
- Heart
- Don Henley
- Whitney Houston
- Billy Idol
- Indigo Girls
- INXS
- Iron Maiden
- Waylon Jennings
- Joan Jett
- Billy Joel
- Howard Jones
- Tom Jones
- Journey
- Judas Priest
- The Judds
- Madeline Kahn
- The Kinks
- KISS
- Kool & the Gang
- Kris Kristofferson
- Nathan Lane
- K.D. Lang
- Angela Lansbury
- Cyndi Lauper

- Chris LeDoux
- Huey Lewis and the News
- LL Cool J
- Kenny Loggins
- Patty Loveless
- Patti LuPone
- Madonna
- Bob Marley
- Wynton Marsalis
- Curtis Mayfield
- Paul McCartney
- Reba McEntire
- Bobby McFerrin
- MC Hammer
- Men at Work
- Alan Menken
- Metallica
- Bette Midler
- Ronnie Milsap
- Charles Mingus
- Motley Crue
- Anne Murray
- Naughty by Nature
- Willie Nelson
- Bebe Neuwirth
- Olivia Newton-John
- New Kids on the Block

- Stevie Nicks
- Jessye Norman
- N.W.A.
- Billy Ocean
- Ozzy Osbourne
- Robert Palmer
- The Pointer Sisters
- Alan Parsons Project
- Dolly Parton
- Mandy Patinkin
- Luciano Pavorotti
- Bernadette Peters
- Pet Shop Boys
- Tom Petty
- Pink Floyd
- The Pixies
- The Pointer Sisters
- Poison
- The Police
- The Pretenders
- Prince
- John Prine
- Public Enemy
- Queen
- Bonnie Raitt
- Lou Reed
- R.E.M.

- REO Speedwagon
- Restless Heart
- Lionel Ritchie
- Chita Rivera
- Kenny Rogers
- The Rolling Stones
- Run DMC
- Rush
- Sade
- Salt-N-Pepa
- The Scorpions
- Dan Seals
- Bob Seeger
- Paul Simon
- Simply Red
- The Smiths
- Sonic Youth
- Bruce Springsteen
- Rod Stewart
- George Strait
- Stray Cats
- Styx
- Survivor
- Talking Heads
- Tears for Fears
- Thompson Twins
- Tone Loc

- TOTO
- Pete Townshend
- Randy Travis
- The Tubes
- Tanya Tucker
- Tina Turner
- Traveling Wilburys
- Twisted Sister
- U2
- Luther Vandross
- Van Halen
- Stevie Ray Vaughan
- Velvet Underground
- WHAM
- Whitesnake
- Steve Winwood
- Colm Wilkinson
- Hank Williams, Jr.
- Lucinda Williams
- Stevie Wonder
- Yes
- Dwight Yoakam
- Yo-Yo Ma
- ZZ Top

1990s—The decade saw minimally produced, anti-establishment grunge bands, and gangster rappers enjoying as much success as the overly produced and studio-manufactured pop groups. Powerful female singers topped the charts. Death by drug overdose and assassination were becoming all too common. Popular genres included grunge, alternative/college rock, technotronic, hip-hop, gangster rap, bubblegum pop, boy bands, girl groups, pop-punk, metal, ska, contemporary R&B, country-pop, Britpop, new jack swing, singer-songwriter, and hard rock.

### Popular 1990s Artists:

- 2Pac
- 50 Cent
- 98 Degrees
- Aerosmith
- Christina Aguilera
- Alabama
- Alice in Chains
- Asleep at the Wheel
- Babyface
- Backstreet Boys
- Barenaked Ladies
- Cecelia Bartoli
- Kathleen Battle
- Beastie Boys
- Beck
- Bell Biv DeVoe
- The Black Crowes
- Mary J. Blige

- Blink-182
- Blues Traveler
- Andrea Bocelli
- Bon Jovi
- Boyz II Men
- Brandy
- Sarah Brightman
- Matthew Broderick
- Garth Brooks
- Brooks & Dunn
- Dave Brubek
- Betty Buckley
- Bush
- Kate Bush
- Bjork
- Cake
- Mariah Carey
- Jose Carreras
- Tracy Chapman
- Kristen Chenoweth
- Cher
- Eric Clapton
- Sean Combs/Puff Daddy
- Harry Connick Jr.
- Chick Corea
- Elvis Costello
- The Cranberries

- Sheryl Crow
- Cypress Hill
- Daft Punk
- Ani DiFranco
- Digital Underground
- Dixie Chicks (The Chicks)
- Celine Dion
- Placido Domingo
- Dr. Dre
- Eminem
- En Vogue
- Gloria Estefan
- Melissa Etheridge
- Everclear
- Faith No More
- Harvey Fierstein
- Foo Fighters
- Renee Fleming
- Garbage
- Vince Gill
- Gin Blossoms
- Godsmack
- Goo Goo Dolls
- Green Day
- Guns N' Roses
- Emmylou Harris
- Neil Patrick Harris

- Jeff Healy
- Heart
- Heavy D
- Faith Hill
- Lauryn Hill
- Hootie & the Blowfish
- Whitney Houston
- Dmitri Hvorostovsky
- Ice Cube
- Incubus
- Indigo Girls
- Hugh Jackman
- Janet Jackson
- Alan Jackson
- Michael Jackson
- Jane's Addiction
- Jay-Z
- Waylon Jennings
- Jewel
- Jeremy Jorden
- Madeline Kahn
- Toby Keith
- Korn
- Lenny Kravitz
- Nathan Lane
- K.D. Lang
- Angela Lansbury

- Chris Ledoux
- Annie Lennox
- Live
- Patty Loveless
- Patti LuPone
- Madonna
- Marilyn Manson
- Dave Matthews Band
- MC Hammer
- Wynton Marsalis
- Ricky Martin
- Matchbox 20
- Audra McDonald
- Reba McEntire
- Bobby McFerrin
- Tim McGraw
- Sarah Mclaughlin
- Megadeth
- Alan Menken
- Natalie Merchant
- Metallica
- George Michael
- Alanis Morissette
- Willie Nelson
- Anna Netrebko
- Bebe Neuwirth
- New Edition

- Nine Inch Nails
- Nirvana
- No Doubt
- Jessye Norman
- Notorious B.I.G.
- N' Sync
- N.W.A.
- Oasis
- The Offspring
- Outkast
- Joan Osborne
- Ozzy Osbourne
- Pantera
- Dolly Parton
- Mandy Patinkin
- Pearl Jam
- Bernadette Peters
- Tom Petty
- Liz Phair
- Phish
- Pink
- Primus
- The Pixies
- Prince
- John Prine
- Public Enemy
- Queen Latifa

- Radiohead
- Bonnie Raitt
- R.E.M.
- Red Hot Chili Peppers
- LeAnn Rimes
- Run DMC
- Lea Salonga
- Salt 'n Peppa
- Smashing Pumpkins
- Smashmouth
- Snoop Dogg
- Sonic Youth
- Soul Asylum
- Slipknot
- Soundgarden
- Britney Spears
- Sting
- Stone Temple Pilots
- George Strait
- Sublime
- SWV
- System of a Down
- Tempe of the Dog
- Third Eye Blind
- TLC
- Toad the Wet Sprocket
- Tone Loc

- Tool
- Randy Travis
- Shania Twain
- U2
- Vanilla Ice
- Stevie Ray Vaughn
- The Verve
- Weezer
- Kanye West
- LeeAnn Womack
- White Zombie
- Lucinda Williams
- Trisha Yearwood
- Dwight Yoakam
- Yo-Yo Ma

2000s—Much of the pop music from the 1990s was reflected in the new millennium, with many of those artists remaining relevant. The 2000s saw 9/11, war, and an economic downturn. Music reflected the grief of these events while also promoting encouragement and optimism. Popular genres included dance-pop, indie rock, emo, pop-punk, contemporary R&B, hip-hop, reggaeton, electronica, hard rock, alternative metal, new wave revival, teen pop, boy bands, internet stars, Disney artists, adult contemporary, country, country-pop, British soul, and Latin pop.

*Popular 2000s Artists:*

- 3 Doors Down
- 50 Cent
- Aaliyah

- Ryan Adams
- Adele
- Christina Aguilera
- The All American Rejects
- Asleep at the Wheel
- Cecelia Bartoli
- Beyoncé
- Justin Bieber
- Blink-182
- Andrea Bocelli
- Michelle Branch
- Matthew Broderick
- Brooks & Dunn
- Bjork
- Colbie Caillat
- Mariah Carey
- Jose Carreras
- Kenny Chesney
- Eric Church
- Eric Clapton
- Kelly Clarkson
- Les Claypool
- Coldplay
- Sean Combs/Puff Daddy
- Miley Cyrus
- Destiny's Child
- Dixie Chicks (The Chicks)

- Drake
- Eminem
- Evanescence
- Fall Out Boy
- Five For Fighting
- The Flaming Lips
- Renee Fleming
- Flo Rida
- Fuel
- Renee Elise Goldsberry
- Goo Goo Dolls
- Josh Groban
- Jonathan Groff
- Gorillaz
- Ben Harper
- Emmylou Harris
- Neil Patrick Harris
- PJ Harvey
- Jeff Healy
- Dmitri Hvorostovsky
- Interpol
- Hugh Jackman
- Jack Johnson
- Jay-Z
- The Jonas Brothers
- Norah Jones
- Jeremy Jordan

- Toby Keith
- Alicia Keys
- Kid Rock
- The Killers
- Korn
- Alison Krauss
- Kreator
- Lady Gaga
- Miranda Lambert
- Nathan Lane
- Avril Lavigne
- John Legend
- Lil Wayne
- Linkin Park
- Jennifer Lopez
- Patti LuPone
- Maroon 5
- Wynton Marsalis
- John Mayer
- Audra McDonald
- Tim McGraw
- Alan Menken
- Idina Menzel
- Jessie Mueller
- Muse
- My Chemical Romance
- Nas

- Willie Nelson
- Anna Netrebko
- Bebe Neuwirth
- Nickelback
- Kelli O'Hara
- Outkast
- Brad Paisley
- Panic! At The Disco
- Paramore
- Dolly Parton
- Mandy Patinkin
- Sean Paul
- Pearl Jam
- Katy Perry
- Phish
- Pink
- John Prine
- Radiohead
- Red Hot Chili Peppers
- Rihanna
- Travis Scott
- Shakira
- Blake Shelton
- The Shins
- Jessica Simpson
- Snoop Dogg
- Britney Spears

- Regina Spektor
- Staind
- Joss Stone
- The Strokes
- Taylor Swift
- System of a Down
- Justin Timberlake
- Tool
- Train
- A Tribe Called Quest
- U2
- Umphrey's McGee
- Carrie Underwood
- Usher
- Velvet Revolver
- Kanye West
- The White Stripes
- Lucinda Williams
- Amy Winehouse
- LeeAnn Womack

2010s—Music streaming became conventional. A variety of styles continued to emerge, including "whisperpop," characterized by subdued vocals, muted notes, and breath intensity. Singer-songwriters and indie rock musicians integrated mandolin, dulcimer, ukulele, bongos, and accordion. Adult contemporary music was very successful, incorporating soul, rock, and folk into pop music. Popular genres included rock, alternative, psychedelic rock, progressive and experimental rock, pop punk, punk rock, hard rock, heavy metal, pop rock, contemporary R&B and soul, hip-hop, electronic, country, and Christian.

### *Popular 2010s Artists:*

- 5 Seconds of Summer
- 21 Savage
- Adele
- Jason Aldean
- Sara Bareilles
- Dierks Bentley
- Beyoncé
- Justin Bieber
- Big Sean
- The Black-Eyed Peas
- Andrea Bocelli
- Chris Brown
- BTS
- Luke Bryan
- Michael Bublé
- Camila Cabello
- Colbie Caillat
- Alessia Cara
- Cardi B.
- Chance the Rapper
- The Chainsmokers
- Eric Church
- Kelly Clarkson

- J. Cole
- Coldplay
- Luke Combs
- Darren Criss
- Miley Cyrus
- Drake
- Billie Eilish
- Renee Fleming
- Florence + The Machine
- Flo Rida
- Florida Georgia Line
- Future
- Renee Elise Goldsberry
- Selena Gomez
- Andy Grammar
- Ariana Grande
- CeeLo Green
- Josh Groban
- Jonathan Groff
- Gucci Mane
- Halsey
- Calvin Harris
- Imagine Dragons
- Jay-Z
- Vance Joy
- Juice Wrld
- Khalid

- DJ Khaled
- Kesha
- Kodak Black
- Lady Antebellum (Lady A)
- Lady Gaga
- Ellie Goulding
- David Guetta
- Neil Patrick Harris
- Sam Hunt
- Alan Jackson
- Toby Keith
- Kendrick Lamar
- Mirada Lambert
- John Legend
- Lil Wayne
- Little Big Town
- Lizzo
- LMFAO
- Logic
- Lorde
- Demi Lovato
- The Lumineers
- Machine Gun Kelly
- Macklemore & Ryan Lewis
- Maroon 5
- Bruno Mars
- John Mayer

- Ava Max
- Tim McGraw
- Shawn Mendes
- Alan Menken
- Lea Michelle
- Migos
- Mac Miller
- Nicki Minaj
- Lin Manuel Miranda
- Jason Mraz
- Jessie Mueller
- Mumford & Sons
- Kacey Musgraves
- Anna Netrebko
- NF
- Leslie Odom Jr.
- Kelli O'Hara
- One Direction
- One Republic
- Brad Paisley
- Panic! At The Disco
- Pentatonix
- Christina Perri
- Katy Perry
- Pink
- Pitbull
- Ben Platt

- Post Malone
- John Prine
- Charlie Puth
- Anthony Ramos
- Lana Del Rey
- Thomas Rhett
- Rhianna
- Travis Scott
- Ed Sheeran
- Blake Shelton
- Sam Smith
- Sia
- Phillipa Soo
- Trey Songz
- Chris Stapleton
- Hailee Steinfeld
- Taylor Swift
- Chris Stapleton
- Justin Timberlake
- Train
- Meghan Trainor
- twenty one pilots
- Carrie Underwood
- Keith Urban
- The Weeknd
- Kanye West
- Pharrell Williams

- XXXTentacion
- Young Chop
- Young Thug
- The Zac Brown Band

Research indicates that the music of our young adulthood—high school/early 20s—is the music that sticks with us our entire lives. What decade is *your* music? Do you agree with that assessment? Whether you do or not, you're likely listening to that music through digital means. Check out this 2020 breakdown of digital music sales by genre:

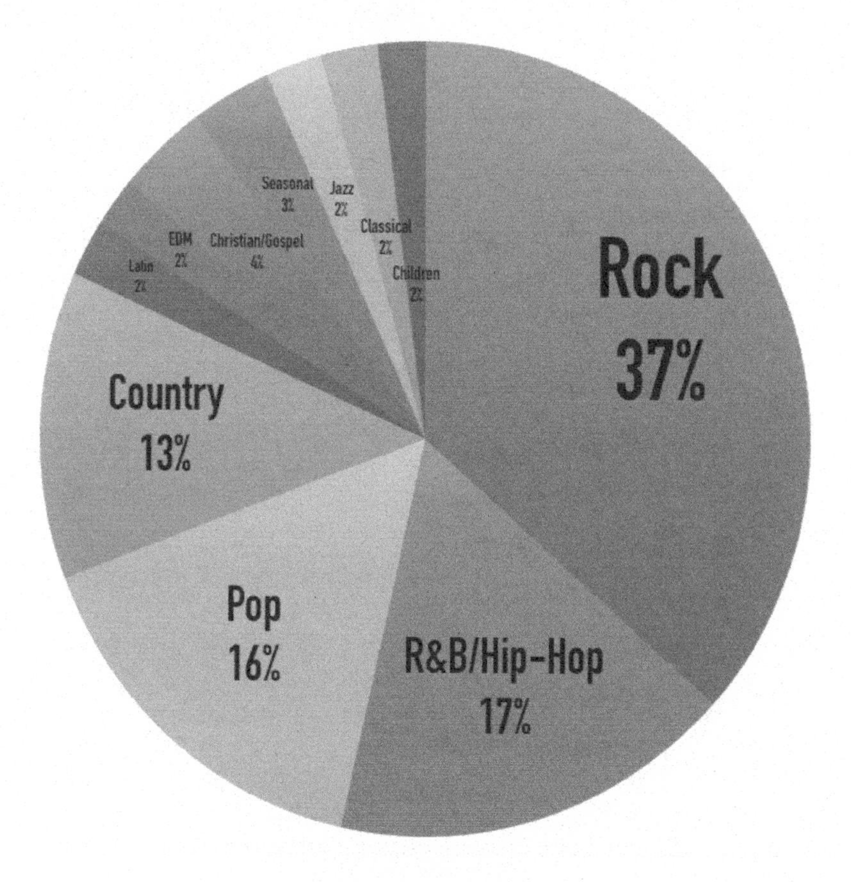


(Digital Music News, 2021)

Technology's advancement has been revolutionary, and it seems no audio format will live forever. We now and for the foreseeable future exist in the digital age. Most music consumers—that's us—have evolved to streaming. The question bears asking, how will streaming change us?

## A Nod to the Ladies: Women Rocking the Industry

From the covert composer to the punk powerhouse to the pop princess, women have always rocked. Hard.

Very little mention is made of women in classical music up through the beginning of the twentieth century. While there were many female contributors to classical music—the popular music from the twelfth century to the early 1900s—they don't get a whole lot of credit. There is some mention of Hildegard of Bingen (1098-1179), Barbara Strozzi (1619-64), Fanny Mendelssohn Hensel (1805-47), Ethel Smyth (1858-1944), Rebecca Clarke (1886-1979), Lili Boulanger (1893-1918), and Elizabeth Maconchy (1907-94). Perhaps the most well-known woman of classical music is Clara Schumann (1819-96), a composer and pianist, who is best known in the context of supporting her composer husband, Robert Schumann. *The Encyclopedia of Classical Music*, published in 1999, mentions only sixteen women. The men outnumber them by nearly four hundred.

Even if they managed to acquire a basic music education, women were barred from jobs in the music profession for centuries. They were also excluded from the societies and networks that gave male composers important contacts and opportunities. A woman's place was in the home, although some young women were encouraged to learn an instrument, sing, or attempt composing. Such accomplishments, however, were only displayed to family and friends. Public exposure, including publication, was considered shameful. (Robert, 1999)

Fast forward to the twentieth century. N'Gai Croal wrote in a 2001 *Newsweek* article, titled "Music: Ladies with Attitude," about how difficult it is to be a woman in pop music. Croal mentioned how every so often, a few break through, such as Annie Lennox, Madonna, and Lauryn Hill. "Occasionally, enough will break through at roughly the same time that critics will opine about a 'Women in Rock' revolution, as in the mid-1990s when Hole, Liz Phair, P.J. Harvey, and Alanis Morissette were among the most exciting acts on the scene." But for the most part, Croal said much of the industry's emphasis is on the look, not the music. The industry seems more comfortable with the girls who are spilling out of their hot pink shorts or baring their midriffs. Croal suggested that posing in a slip on the cover of *Rolling Stone* is the best way to promote yourself. She also said women are more easily controlled than men, especially in the music business, and after the market-imposed three-album term limits, they are easily disposed of and recreated, like "fembots," with this year's model. Croal said the anti-formula for all of this is the bad girl persona. A "rock-ish, I-just-don't-give-a-damn sneer" and/or or a scandalous personal history will guarantee a lifetime membership in the "Bad Girl Club."

Eric Danton reprised this philosophy in a 2003 *Sydney Morning Herald* article, titled "Can girls save rock 'n' roll? Not while their lip gloss gets more attention than their guitar licks." Danton discussed how women get more press for their girly looks than for their musical ability and are more often described as sexy instead of as rockers. He also said that woman-fronted bands, such as No Doubt and Garbage, have assumed a more prominent position in the industry than solo female performers and all-female groups. "Talented women in garage rock bands are writing the same kinds of loud, unpretentious, stripped-down songs that have earned accolades for their male counterparts," Danton said. "But rock has always been a boys' club—mostly male bands playing to mostly male audiences where women are along for the ride.... There have been exceptions over the years, of course. The women in the Runaways, the Go-Gos, and Sleater-Kinney, among others, rock as hard as any men."

"She's a rebel: The history of women in rock & roll," by Gillian Gaar (2002) chronicled a half century of women performers including the early R&B singers, girl groups, and Motown acts of the fifties, the folk singers and rock chicks of the sixties, the punk rebels and disco divas of the seventies, and the all-girl bands, rappers, hip-hoppers, and riot girls who shook the music world from the eighties into the new century. Gaar said women in rock have been a perpetual trend, but they are still by and large defined in that order—as women first, and rock performers second. They are typically identified, for example, as the "best female guitarist" as opposed to the "best guitarist." If women performers (or songwriters, DJs, managers, etc.) are only seen as exceptional because they are women, there is a relegation of women, as their contributions are acknowledged but are also portrayed as being a step removed from the history as a whole. The implication is that women in rock make an impression in spite of the fact that they are female. This perpetuates stereotypical views regarding women's capabilities to be anything other than the most passive kind of entertainers. However, there has been a substantial increase in the visibility of women in the rock world, even if women in rock are still presented as something of a novelty. And though the executive suites in the music industry remain male-dominated, women continue to move into other areas of the business.

Gaar broke down the evolution of women in popular music into the following categories:

### THE ROOTS (1940s & 1950s)

Big Mama Thornton, Ruth Brown, LaVern Baker, Etta James, Lady Bo, Bonnie Guitar, Wanda Jackson, The Bobbettes, The Chantels

### GIRL GROUPS (early to mid-1960s)

The Shirelles, The Chiffons, Ellie Greenwich, The Shangri-Las, The Crystals, The Ronettes, Darlene Love, Lesley Gore, Dusty Springfield, Vicki Wickham, Carol MacDonald/Goldie and the Gingerbreads

## REVOLUTION (mid- to late 1960s)

Mary Wells, Martha Reeves & the Vandellas, The Supremes, Aretha Franklin, Tina Turner, Joan Baez, Janis Joplin, Maureen Tucker/Velvet Underground, Alison Steele

## HEAR ME ROAR (early to mid-1970s)

Helen Reddy, Cris Williamson, Pamela Brandt/Deadly Nightshade, June Millington/Fanny, Holly Near, Teresa Trull, Karen Carpenter

## DIVERSE DIRECTIONS (1970s)

Carole King, Laura Nyro, Joni Mitchell, Bonnie Raitt, Joan Armatrading, Labelle, Donna Summer, The Runaways, Heart

## PUNK REVOLUTION (mid-1970s to mid-1980s)

Yoko Ono, Patti Smith, X-Ray Spex, Siouxsie & the Banshees, Nina Hagen, Lene Lovich, Marianne Faithfull, Debbie Harry/Blondie, Penelope Spheeris, Exene Cervenka/X, Kate Bush

## POST-PUNK WAVES (1980s)

Go-Gos, Chrissie Hynde/The Pretenders, Pat Benatar, Danielle Dax, Laurie Anderson, Karen Finley

## SMILE FOR THE CAMERA (1980s)

Annie Lennox/Eurythmics, Cyndi Lauper, Madonna, Joan Jett, The Bangles, Whitney Houston

## STEP INTO THE FUTURE (late 1980s to early 1990s)

Suzanne Vega, Tracy Chapman, Michelle Shocked, Phranc, k.d. lang, Sinead O'Connor, Janet Jackson, Gloria Estefan/Miami Sound Machine, Lita Ford, Vixen, Salt-N-Pepa, Queen Latifah, Diamanda Galas

## ENJOY BEING A GRRRL (1990s)

Throwing Muses, Kim Gordon, Bikini Kill, Bratmobile/Riot Grrrl, Breeders, L7, Babes in Toyland, Courtney Love/Hole

## NEW PERSPECTIVES (1990s to early 2000s)

Liz Phair, Tori Amos, Alanis Morissette, Sheryl Crow, Sarah McLachlan/ Lilith Fair, Natalie Merchant, Jewel, PJ Harvey, Bjork, Mary J. Blige, En Vogue, TLC, Ani DiFranco, Sleater-Kinney

## GIRL POWER (late 1990s to early 2000s)

Spice Girls, Britney Spears, Gwen Stefani/No Doubt, Mariah Carey, Macy Gray, Alicia Keys, Lauryn Hill, Destiny's Child, Missy Elliott, Lucinda Williams, Kirsty MacColl, Laura Love, Ladyfest, The Donnas

If you're interested in more on the ladies, I highly recommend *Rolling Stone* music journalist Gerri Hirshey's (2001) "We gotta get out of this place: The true, tough story of women in rock." Hirshey discussed how rock and roll (and its counterparts in blues, soul, hip-hop, etc.) has traditionally been a boys' game. It has forced female artists to work twice as hard, usually for half the recognition. She said that without their contributions, however, American music would be radically impoverished.

Fifty years before Janis Joplin instructed her stylist to stitch up a handbag big enough for a book and a bottle, blueswoman Ma Rainey—known in her day as the ugliest woman in show business—barnstormed the south in a scrappy wooden trailer latched to a car. Ma stayed on the road for thirty years and had her own essentials: frying pans and feather boas. Despite all her traveling and billing as "Mother of the Blues," Ma's hometown obituary listed her as a housekeeper. Today, women own their own copyrights, record companies, and destinies. They maintain their publishing rights and run their own labels. They keep the domestic hearth burning—and stay on the move. But despite social, economic, political, and technological changes, there are constants as well for women in music, including their escape from the stereotypes of womanhood.

Too often, the industry measures a woman's journey in units sold, tickets bought, and the frequency of website hits. In the final two years of the twentieth century, the big news was that after all these long, strange trips, women have arrived. But in reality, women have been at the heart of rock and roll all along. They were wailing at rock's beginning, in its blues and gospel ancestry. They have had their sounds and looks arranged by the marketing plans of men. At other moments, they have been held forth in the boldest spotlights. "They've been worshipped and objectified, over-dubbed and underpaid. Like their male counterparts, they can be deeply passionate or chillingly calculated. But they have never—ever—been quiet" (Hirshey, 2001). By millennium's end, women were everywhere in music. Their ascent was loud and immensely profitable, and they weren't going away. Divas, new and reincarnated, were dominant—and marketable.

Taken as a whole, the narrative of women in rock amounts to "a sort of cultural travelogue, fraught with bandstand suffrage and pillow talk, gender wars and loving cease-fires. What the music has done for people historically disenfranchised—women, and especially black women—is nothing short of miraculous"

Hirshey categorized the evolution of women in rock as the following:

## THE MOTHERS OF INVENTION

LaVerne Baker, Ruth Brown, Maybelle Carter, June Carter Cash, Patsy Cline, Ella Fitzgerald, Billie Holiday, Lena Horne, Mahalia Jackson, Wanda Jackson, Etta James, Peggy Lee, Ma Rainey, Bessie Smith, Sweet Mama Stringbean, Sister Rosetta Tharpe, Big Mama Thornton, Sarah Vaughan, Dinah Washington

## THE '60s: FROM SHOOP SHOOP TO LADY SOUL

Joan Baez, Cher, Chiffons, Petula Clark, Judy Collins, Crystals, Marianne Faithfull, Connie Francis, Aretha Franklin, Lesley Gore, Cissy Houston,

Janis Joplin, Gladys Knight (& the Pips), Joni Mitchell, Laura Nyro, Martha Reeves & the Vandellas, Ronettes, Diana Ross, Shangri-Las, Shirelles, Nina Simone, Grace Slick, Ronnie Spector, Dusty Springfield, Supremes, Tina Turner, Dionne Warwick, Mary Wells

## THE '70s: SIRENS, PUNKS, AND DISCO QUEENS

Cher, Exene Cervenka, Aretha Franklin, Gloria Gaynor, Emmylou Harris, Debbie Harry/Blondie, Chrissie Hynde, Rickie Lee Jones, Chaka Khan, Carole King, Gladys Knight, Labelle, Bette Midler, Joni Mitchell, Stevie Nicks, Dolly Parton, Linda Ronstadt, Diana Ross, Carly Simon, Siouxsie Sioux, Sister Sledge, Patti Smith, Poly Styrene, Donna Summer, Wendy O. Williams

## THE '80s: PROVOCATEURS, BOY TOYS, AND FIERCE MCS

Joan Armatrading, B-52's, Bananarama, Bangles, Pat Benatar, Edie Brickell, Tracy Chapman, Shawn Colvin, Melissa Etheridge, Go-Go's, Heart, Whitney Houston, Janet Jackson, Joan Jett, Cyndi Lauper, Annie Lennox, Madonna, Natalie Merchant, Stevie Nicks, Sinead O'Connor, Bonnie Raitt, Salt 'N Pepa, Tina Turner, Suzanne Vega

## THE '90s: RIOT GRRLS AND MACK MAMAS, TROUBADOURS, AND PISSED OFF HIPPIE SPAWN

Tori Amos, Fiona Apple, Erykah Badu, Bikini Kill, Mary J. Blige, Brandy, Toni Braxton, Mariah Carey, Sheryl Crow, Ani DiFranco, Celine Dion, Dixie Chicks, Missy Elliott, En Vogue, Melissa Etheridge, Kim Gordon, P.J. Harvey, Faith Hill, Lauryn Hill, Whitney Houston, Janet Jackson, Luscious Jackson, Jewel, L7, k.d. lang, Queen Latifah, Lil' Kim, Courtney Love/Hole, Madonna, Sarah McLachlan, Monica, Alanis Morissette, Liz Phair, LeAnn Rimes, Riot Grrl, Veruca Salt, Michelle Shocked, TLC, Shania Twain

## DAY OF THE DIVAS

Mary J. Blige, Brandy, Mariah Carey, Cher, Celine Dion, Gloria Estefan, Faith Evans, Aretha Franklin, Whitney Houston, Chaka Kahn, Jenny Lind,

Courtney Love, Madonna, LeAnn Rhimes, Diana Ross, Barbra Streisand, Tina Turner

### THE ANTI-DIVAS: PO-MO MAMAS AND HEAVEN-SENT BITCHES

Mary J. Blige, Cibo Matto, Destiny's Child, Missy Elliott, Macy Gray, Lauryn Hill, Lil' Kim, Laura Nyro, Sleater-Kinney, Angie Stone, TLC, Lucinda Williams

In the first two decades of the twenty-first century, women have continued to make their mark on rock history and are closing the gender gap in the music industry's current climate. Here are a few girl power-inspired conclusions from my research:

- Women's role in the history of popular music is more cyclical than linear, and much of their progress can be associated with social and political trends. For example, several women emerged on the music scene during the second wave of feminism, when women were getting out of the house. They were no longer limited by wife and mother roles and could now have careers, income, and autonomy. Third wave feminism added the elements of race, class, and sexual orientation, which can all be seen in the evolution of women in popular music.
- The music industry is a policy-making institution with an economic infrastructure, although the industry does not always represent popular preference and what popular culture defines as mainstream. If you compare *Billboard Magazine's* record sales and public demand to Grammy award winners, you will find a lot of discrepancies. Same goes in comparing the Grammy's to the People's Choice-type awards. The decision-makers and the people are not synonymous.
- While music genres are fluid and permeable, it seems that genres outside of rock—specifically, jazz, country, folk, and opera—are

more acceptable for women. However, these other musical traditions seem to accept women more as "vocalists" than as "musicians."

- Women influence and perpetuate popular culture, very much so in the music industry. Women consume popular culture, as evidenced not only by purchasing the music, but also by consuming the fashion and the image. Remember all the young girls who bought lacey tops and bangles and transformed their hair to look just like Madonna in the eighties?
- Women in music oppose patriarchy by taking control and establishing their own power. In the binary opposition of men versus women, some women respond by mimicking and assimilating. Others innovate.
- Considering the ideal of maternalism—women in music do not have to choose career OR motherhood. Many choose both. Liz Phair took a hiatus from the industry to focus on motherhood and family. She suffered no backlash. One of the Dixie Chicks was in her third trimester of pregnancy in their *Landslide* video. Her baby didn't slow her down or change the band. Pink brings her entire family along on tour.
- Women in popular music are definitely sex positive, especially today with so much sexuality in their lyrics and image. The public is seeing a lot of packaged music and sex. Comparing women in music today to the Miss America Pageant, talent is certainly taken more seriously. That is because it is presented in a different context. However, when you attach the glam, the beauty—"feminine" attributes to a female musician, such as Britney Spears, her music is not taken as seriously and she loses credibility. Her image gets more attention than her music (not to mention her personal drama). And the audience certainly doesn't consider any social criticism or representation in her music, as opposed to

someone like Ani DiFranco, whose dreadlocks and tattoos seem to make her a more acceptable spokesperson for feminism. (I must admit that I glam myself up a bit when my band performs. I wear sluttier clothes and more make-up. My hair is bigger. This is not so much about projecting a pretty image, though. I simply feel more confident when I'm more decked out and that's important when performing. Of course, I show up to rehearsals in a T-shirt, jeans, and ponytail. The guys don't seem to mind.)

- Are women in music role models? Not so much as women in sports. Athletes project an image of good health, perseverance, and strength. However, despite the psychological and physical perseverance, strength, and stamina necessary in the music business, the overall image of rock is more connected to an unhealthy lifestyle of drugs and alcohol, promiscuity, unseemly travel, and living fast and hard. Rock stars are not considered grounded or domestic. They inhabit a male space, their class and status are to be reckoned with, and everyone has a vice. The pop star image, as opposed to the rock star image, is different though. Dua Lipa is chastised for dressing too risqué and for the message she may be sending to her primary audience of young girls. Hard-core rockers do not seem to get as much backlash, maybe because the message in their music is somewhat reflected in their image. So why do we beat up the pop stars when their message is much more benign? And why don't men in music have to contend with this image crap? Women must be much more conscious of their decisions and actions—and image. Kudos to beautiful, unapologetic artists like Meghan Trainor and Lizzo who love themselves and their size and honestly couldn't care less about the trolls.
- There are several commonalities among women in music, especially with the pioneers and trailblazers in the industry: an attitude of determination, a proactive perspective, perseverance, confidence, independence, and establishing and defining their

own roles in the industry. Many women now own and run their own record labels—and retain the rights and profits to their songs, which has put them in a position of power. And the more marginalized (less mainstream) the music, the more control women have. In challenging the pop market, their audience isn't the mass audience—they are more diverse and less homogenized. Success isn't always measured by profit, but women today are commanding the respect and the higher salaries they deserve.

- Women can be strong, independent, raw, sexual, and vulnerable. Feminism, in the context of women in rock, is about changing rules and doing things for yourself and other women on your own terms. Much of the feminist text is now in the music itself. Defiance, sexual revenge, and issues of trauma are all in the lyrics.

I am personally grateful to these women for paving this road and creating opportunities for musicians like myself. My band continues to be a tremendous source of stress relief, creative release, and personal catharsis. For the first twenty years we jammed, I was the lead singer—and the only girl. Being one of the guys is something I treasure in those social relationships. I have always felt like an absolute equal. Almost to the extreme, sometimes. Nobody ever helped me schlep my eighty-lb. keyboard and amp unless I asked. So much for chivalry. (Maybe it's because I can belch them all under the table.)

In the next chapter, we move from music history to music's effects on the brain and body. The science is real. The advantages are ginormous.

# III. DEVELOPMENT

*"Don't know much about history. Don't know much biology. Don't know much about a science book. Don't know much about the French I took. But I do know that I love you. And I know that if you love me too, what a wonderful world this would be." —Sam Cooke*

The musical experience is a behavior, which involves both making and receiving music. This comprises listening, performance, improvisation, and composition. Performance alone is a multifaceted behavior involving motor skills, proprioception, kinesthetics, sensory integration, emotional memory, intellect, and creativity. (Crowe, 2004) There's a lot going on here.

You are likely aware of music's multiple benefits from the perspectives of neuroscience, education, psychology, sociology, and health. Regardless of your musical experience or training, you may already be enjoying those benefits.

## YOUR BRAIN ON MUSIC

Music activates every part of the brain and contributes considerably to its neuroplasticity, which is the brain's ability to form and reorganize synaptic connections. It is essentially a massive neuron party (with a DJ, a dance floor, and a disco ball, of course). I am not arrogant enough to call myself a brain expert, but I do know from research and experience that it's all about the endorphins! You know, those happy chemicals that give us a natural high after exercise, sex, dark chocolate, laughter, kindness, sunlight, pets, art, and music (duh).

### We can hack these happy chemicals through music:

- Dopamine (the reward chemical)
- Serotonin (the mood stabilizer)
- Oxytocin (the love/bonding hormone)
- Endorphin (the pain killer)

### Music also stimulates our various brain waves:

- *Delta waves (sleep)* are associated with deepest levels of relaxation, healing, and regeneration.
- *Theta waves (relaxed)* occur during sleep and relaxation and are related to dreams, imagery, and intuition.
- *Alpha waves (calm)* occur when you are awake, but your mind is in a resting state.
- *Beta waves (alert)* occur the most during conscious, waking states.
- *Gamma waves (thinking/working)* are the fastest wavelength brain wave, linked to learning, problem-solving, and information processing.

All that good stuff going on in the brain is clearly conducive to learning too, right? Of course, right! Music classes help students develop and improve musical skills, and increase knowledge of music theory and history. But music can address so many additional areas. Take note:

- *Kids who study music are higher academic achievers in proportional math and fractions, language arts/reading/verbal skills, science, and spatial-temporal (logic/problem-solving) skills. They also have higher self-esteem, stronger emotional health, and better social, leadership, and presentation skills.*
- *When children begin school, the development of their mental capacities continues, while they begin to experience larger social interactions and the demands of schoolwork. Music can play an important role in this stage of life.*
- *Many parallels exist between speech and singing, rhythm and motor behavior, musical mnemonics and rote memorization, and overall ability of preferred music to enhance mood, attention, and behavior to optimize an individual's ability to learn and interact.*
- *Music stimulates all the senses and involves the child at many levels. This multi-modal approach facilitates numerous developmental skills.*
- *Quality learning and maximum participation occur when children are permitted to experience the joy of play. The medium of music enables this play to occur naturally and frequently.*
- *Music is highly motivating, yet it can also have a calming effect. Enjoyable music activities are designed to be success-oriented and make children feel good about themselves.*
- *Music can encourage socialization, self-expression, communication, and motor development. Music can also promote the learning of academic concepts, increase cooperation and appropriate social behavior, provide avenues for communication, increase self-esteem and confidence, and improve motor responses and agility.*

*(NAfME, 2021)*

And that's just for kids, silly rabbit! Music reaches us at all ages, developmental levels, and demographics. In the next chapter, I will further expound on music's influence in all domains of human functioning: developmental, cognitive, communicative, physical, social, psychological/emotional, and spiritual. For now, I am going to focus on the social aspect of music and the brain.

Research published in *American Psychologist* in 2021 provided a neuroscientific understanding of social connection through music. This illustration is a map of the brain when playing music, emphasizing what happens in the brain when people make music together, rather than listening to music individually.

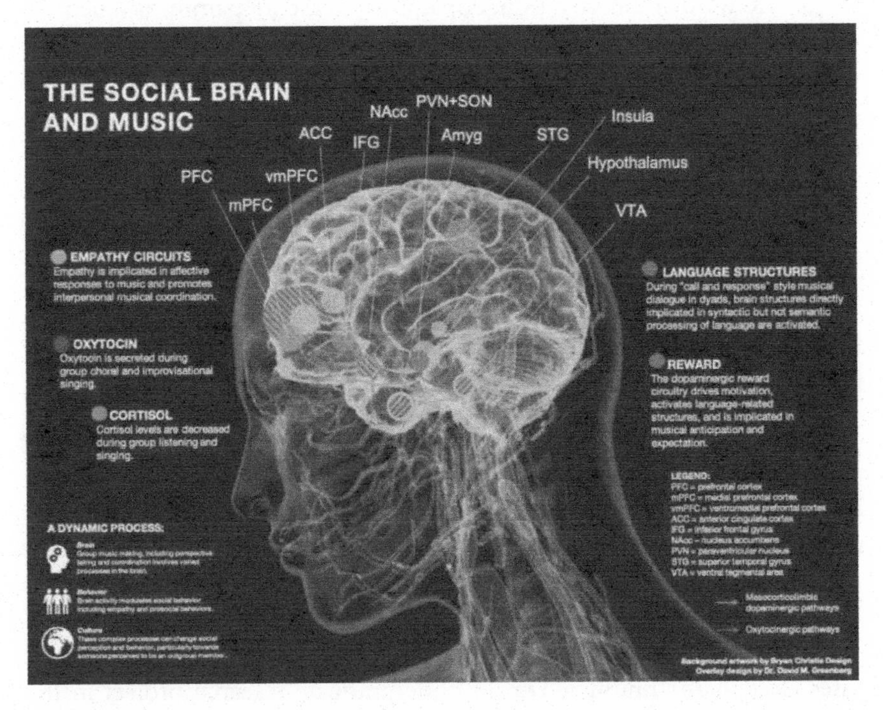


(Greenberg et al., 2021)

The research was inspired by creative efforts of people around the world to make music together while social distancing during the COVID-19 pandemic. This included people singing in unison from balcony to balcony, group singing on video conferencing platforms, and live living room concerts by Yo-Yo Ma and others.

The researchers identified five key functions and mechanisms of the brain that contribute to social connection through music:

1. Empathy circuits (empathy helps us tune in to how others are feeling and can be improved through interpersonal musical coordination)
2. Oxytocin secretion (oxytocin contributes to our sense of belonging and feeling socially bonded with others; it is secreted when people sing together)
3. Reward and motivation; dopamine release (dopamine is a neurotransmitter that produces a sense of pleasure and is released during musical anticipation/expectation; it contributes to a sense of motivation and reward)
4. Language structures (musical dialogue involves language structures in the brain)
5. Cortisol decrease (cortisol is a hormone that contributes to stress; it is decreased in the brain when people sing and listen to music together)

The authors concluded that music is a powerful tool that can bring individuals together, promote empathy and communication, and heal social divisions.

My personal example of music and social connections corroborates Greenberg's findings. For an undergraduate research project in the spring of 2003, I conducted a qualitative study about the benefits of weekly music-making for six busy adults…my band of now twenty-three years, the Salt Rhythm Band (SRB). Qualitative research (narrative/descriptive), as opposed to quantitative research (sadistics—I mean, statistics), often involves the researcher as a participant in the study and is told from first person perspective. Remember, this was written almost twenty years ago. If you jump to the present, the story has evolved a bit, but the early chronicle is pertinent. First, a quick review of the literature.

Some research exists on the benefits of music from an educational perspective and much has been published on the therapeutic benefits of music in various domains, such as cognitive, physical, behavioral, psychological, and social. Sturm (1998), in presenting a history of music advocacy over the past 150 years, found the benefits of music study to include strengthening the individual and community, maintaining a person's physical, emotional, and intellectual well-being, and providing good social and moral influence. O'Toole (2000) argued that a primary reason for music-making is identity affirmation. In a study about the social phenomenology and the ethnographic representation of technology in music-making, Porcello (1998) suggested that recording technology replaces the unified "we-ness" of live music-making.

Pavlicevic (2000) considered improvisation (which plays a large role in SRB's rehearsals) as human communication in sound. The author said music improvisation is understood as a musical event in which skilled musicians play music together in a free, spontaneous manner. Musicians create music together, coordinating with one another rhythmically and melodically, constantly evolving new musical textures. They depend on each other for musical ideas, respond to each other's cues, and communicate with each other musically. Although the event is an original one, it inevitably draws from the players' existing knowledge of musical styles and improvisational techniques. In free improvisation, the presence of predetermined tempo, rhythm, harmonics, and phrasing are minimal. The improvisers together construct a shared context in which a joint repertoire of musical events is created and adapted on the spot. Musicians express themselves and communicate with others through free improvisation. The basis for music improvisation is musical, although it may also generate intense interpersonal intimacy.

Anshel & Kipper (1988) investigated the effects of group singing on trust and cooperation. The authors proposed that music is a universal medium for expressing ideas and emotions, for promoting better interpersonal behavior, communication, identification, confidence, imagination, and self-awareness, and for providing opportunities for catharsis. Results of their study indicate that the elicitation of trust and cooperation requires the type of involvement that combines both music and activity, such as group singing.

Campbell and Heller (1980) said music is a form of human communication and the listener is a perceiver whose responses can be studied within the framework of a psychology of perception. Responses in the form of musical performance could serve as indicators of successful communication.

In an illustration of the behavior of music listeners, Haack (1980) referenced Gaston (1968), who stressed the importance of the social context in the development of man and music. "Music is communication," and is born out of responsive behaviors. "Music is derived from the tender emotions," and is used to evoke and enhance friendly, humane, and loving relationships, feelings of closeness, and caring-sharing behaviors in general. Finally, "The potency of music is greatest in the group." Haack compared Gaston's considerations to Merriam's (1964) ten functions of music, which are emotional expression, aesthetic enjoyment, entertainment, communication, symbolic representation, physical response, enforcing conformity to social norms, validation of social institutions and religious rituals, contribution to the continuity and stability of culture, and contribution to the integration of society.

Looking further at musical behavior, Radocy & Boyle (1988) said it is interhuman, interpersonal, or social. Musical behavior cannot be understood without examination of the social processes involved. They suggested that "Music is truly a social phenomenon, inviting, encouraging, and in some instances almost requiring individuals to participate in group activity. Music is used as a signal to draw people together or as a rallying point around which individuals gather to engage in activities which require group cooperation and consideration." The authors also referenced Gaston, who said music is a source of gratification because "Music provides opportunities for achievement in noncompetitive situations. The self-esteem which results from music accomplishment contributes greatly to an individual's state of well-being."

So how does this relate to my band and me? From SRB's heyday, this is our story.

## THE BENEFITS OF WEEKLY MUSIC-MAKING FOR SIX BUSY ADULTS

In today's busy, hurried, uncertain world, I often find myself wound up in a tight little ball of stress and frustration. I have too much to do and I am constantly struggling with the quantity versus quality issue in my work, as well as my personal life. Stress is a constant. I need a release not only for the stress, but also for the pent-up creative energy that characterizes the carefree, artistic life I would love to be living. Since that is not a reality, I have discovered a weekly treatment for the residue of my busy life: music. More specifically, music-making. Even more specifically, music-making with a fine group of musicians who also happen to be amazing friends.

This group is the Salt Rhythm Band (SRB). I join them every Wednesday night to play rock and roll, blues, and soul. We make a lot of noise, singing and playing from our guts. We laugh, we hug, we laugh some more, we talk about our lives, we talk about the world, we high-five, we laugh louder, and we share a beautiful love of music. Music is the common thread that unites us six busy people into one cohesive unit. Through this union, we have an outlet for stress relief and creative expression. That outlet occurs through a combination of music-making and socialization. I believe these music-based relationships help us maintain our sanity, and blossom as artists and human beings. These benefits are important for consideration in musical, personal, interpersonal, and professional contexts.

The participants in the study are the six members of SRB. All band members are American, Caucasian, college-educated, lower- to upper-middle class and between the ages of thirty-three and fifty-one. There are five men and one woman. Chris (drums and percussion), who hosts the band's weekly rehearsals, is an engineer with a wife and two sons. Steve (guitar and vocals) is also an engineer—he and Chris met at their workplace (Honeywell)—with a wife and a grown son. Jim (guitar) is a sales representative who recently returned to school to take his career in the geographical mapping direction, and is married with two stepchildren. Dan (bass and vocals) is preparing to graduate from ASU with an accounting degree, and is recently married. Michael (drums and percussion) is an architect with a wife and three daughters. I, Julie, (lead vocals and keyboard) am a public relations/media professional turned music therapist-in-training, and am also recently married. As the researcher and simultaneously, the lead singer of the band, I am a full participant in this study.

The site of the study is the SRB rehearsal studio, which is in an affluent area of East Mesa, AZ. It is a beautiful, quiet area and the house is at the end of the street with a vacant house next door, which means the band can make plenty of noise at little risk of offending the neighbors. The studio itself is a converted garage behind Chris' home. The studio is 500 square feet with carpet on the floor and carpet padding on the walls for sound insulation. The room contains a complete drum set, a complete percussion set with congas, bongos, timbales, cymbals, and various loose percussion instruments, a full-sized keyboard with a small keyboard rigged above it, several speakers and amps, sound boards, a full stereo, a pool table, a television, a mini refrigerator, and shelves littered with hardware materials, tools, books, and boxes. There are pockets of space in the room that are filled once the musicians arrive with their equipment, which includes several guitars and bass guitars, my Rock & Roll Hall of Fame tote bag, Jim's Fender lunchbox, music stands, and coolers.

Artwork adorns the walls and includes an ASU Sparky Budweiser neon sign, a peculiar contemporary painting, the quintessential dogs-playing-poker velvet painting, and a variety of random drawings and magazine pages. A dry-erase board lists songs the band is currently working on and target dates for projects to be completed. What stands out the most in the studio's décor is the plethora of photographs, which partially wallpaper the room. At least fifty pictures, randomly arranged on the walls, illustrate the great camaraderie among this group. Pictures from rehearsals, performances, camping trips, parties, etc. tell a colorful story about the connection within this group that goes far beyond musical.

This qualitative study sought insight into why these individuals fit band into their busy schedules, and the perceived personal and group benefits of their participation. The author, a full participant in the study, conducted two observations, an intensive group interview, and various other methods of data collection and analysis. Following are the findings.

The members of SRB make time for weekly music-making to relieve stress, to improve musical skills, to party and enjoy the camaraderie, and to experience a creative outlet. The band members themselves agreed on their perceived benefits of participation. Jim and Dan, in jest, said it's for "the beer!" Chris summarized it nicely when he said it is "for the groove, creativity, I think there is a release part of it—stress relief, but I think it's the… striving to play better. We've been getting into some grooves that have been really tight, really quality stuff. The challenge is the excitement of making some really good music."

In the group interview discussion, I said, "Another reason for me is that in my everyday musical world, between going to school and going to work, I'm doing all this serious and traditional standard literature. I want to get funky. That's why I come to practice, to do something totally different, that's not so structured, and to exercise different skills, and to make noise. It's fun to make noise!" Jim added to this, "You mix it all in," referring to the different styles and progressions I have learned through school that I practice with the band. Chris said, "I like that. You expose us to different stuff."

Many of these obvious benefits were further confirmed in my interviews with the members' spouses. Chris' wife Julene said, "It's a big source of stress relief for him and something he really looks forward to every week." Jim's wife Mary said the band "gets him out of the house and he's doing what he loves." My husband Steve said, "SRB is a great artistic outlet for Julie. It's a chance to congregate and reinforce friendships with a great group of people. It's fun and healthy."

There was unanimous agreement that we have become better musicians through our band experience. Several participants commented that we have all improved individually in our musical ability and performance. There was also discussion about how we have improved as a cohesive unit. Our musicianship and respect for dynamics have evolved tremendously. We listen and respond to each more effectively than in the past and it carries through in our jams and performances. Much of the band rehearsal is dedicated to improvisational jams, based on one member's contribution of a chord progression, lick, or style. The band is also working on several original tunes. In rehearsing newer material, the band starts and stops several times to get entrances just right. Then we plow straight through the songs, bypassing mistakes. After a song ends, we discuss and correct mistakes and play the song again. Overall, there is a very loose structure in the rehearsal, with no clear leader. Typically, when a new song is being practiced, the person who initiated the song leads the group. That person is responsible for ownership of the song, meaning they provide audio, chart up the chord progression, copy it for the group, and direct it. When the band plays a song they already know, the drummer counts it in and the band takes off with it. I informally conduct, cueing solos, dynamic changes, and stops. There is no set list or agenda for songs from the group's standard repertoire; songs are usually called out and played at random.

Objectively speaking, the band has a very good overall sound. When we are in sync with each other, we play tightly and musically with varying dynamics. When we are not, things fall apart. We laugh at ourselves, though, and challenge ourselves to concentrate, do better, and continue making progress. Our varying musical backgrounds and skill levels are not apparent in performance. If anyone plays their instrument more proficiently than someone else, an audience member would never know the difference. We blend well with our instruments, although we have a tendency to play too loudly. Someone usually calls out the violator and he plays more quietly—temporarily. We have a diverse and complimentary mix of musical tastes, styles, and interpretations and we enjoy playing everything in our eclectic repertoire.

Beyond these obvious benefits of participation in the band, two areas emerged stronger than anything else: the social aspect and the experience of catharsis. Considering socialization, we have been together for five years as the band is currently configured. Three of the members (Chris, Dan, and Steve) have been making music together since 1989. We all connected through friends of friends and several members have come and gone for various reasons (other time commitments, moving away, new interests, etc.). The dynamics of our personal lives vary and we are completely different people. Some of our distinctive personality characteristics often emerge in rehearsals. While this does nobody justice in describing their multi-dimensional characters, Steve is cynical; Dan is rigid; Jim is lackadaisical; Michael is flaky; Chris is laid-back; and I'm obnoxious. Despite our differences, we do have a lot in common and we all share a beautiful love of music that has also brought us together as friends. The six members of SRB are much more than a weekly group. Music and socialization go hand in hand. We have an annual "Party in the Pines" at Chris' property in Vernon, AZ, which is a three-day musical camping commune over Labor Day weekend. This involves setting up a stage with a generator for formal performances by SRB and group jams with guests. An unplugged set typically follows until the wee hours of the morning, in a circle around the campfire with guitars, percussion instruments, and singing. Party in the Pines includes family and friends and over the years has grown from about twenty people to over a hundred. We also have an annual "Festivus" holiday party at the studio and other gatherings throughout the year. SRB performs at Steve's annual block party in Ahwatukee, AZ. Steve also hosts a semi-annual "Freaky Friday" at Apache Lake, which is a two-day to week-long camping and boating trip. Music on the boat and unplugged campfire sets are always highlights. One-day or overnight trips to Saguaro Lake are an abbreviated version of Apache Lake festivities. Whenever this group is together, whether it's the whole gang or only two of us, a guitar comes out, a cooler becomes a drum, and we're making music. An impromptu jam at Jim's Memorial Day swim party and our informal performance at Dan's wedding reception became important memories. From a full band set-up to a harmonica and a tambourine, we bring the music element to any and all social gatherings.

Socialization is a large part of every band rehearsal. Each member arrives between 7:30 and 8:15 to a hearty welcome with hugs and enthusiastic handshakes all around. As we set up our equipment, we chit-chat about last weekend's camping trip and the week's events in the world and at home. Chris' wife Julene drops in to visit and listen. During actual rehearsal, all are serious when the situation calls for it, but are more consistently upbeat, friendly, silly, and light. Even the small victories, such as solidifying a scattered ending, are worthy of celebration with this group! Throughout the evening, considerable quantities of naughty things are consumed with an excess of fist bumps, cheers, and belly laughs. Enthusiastic socializing occurs in between songs, with a great deal of talking over each other and interrupting. At 10:45, the evening is by no means over. After the closing jam, we pack up our equipment and load up our cars. Then we return to listen to some more music (some for general listening and some for considering as new tunes to learn) and play pool. This is wind-down time, as everyone relaxes and sobers up to head home. We leave one by one, again with hugs and handshakes all around.

To share some perspectives from the band members, Jim said, "We camp together and we play together." Steve said, "We all love music and alcohol!" I said, "It's also for the camaraderie and the friendship and the once-a-week party." Dan said, "I like having you guys as friends and I can act stupid without feeling too bad about it!"

SRB frequently invites guest musicians to jam with us. Our regulars include musicians on trumpet, harmonica, guitar, bass, fiddle, banjo, mandolin, vocals, and keyboards. Many of our parties involve guests joining us on stage and relieving us for breaks. These guests always have a great time and unreservedly express their appreciation. Our collaboration with them is of great benefit to SRB, as well. We have improved our musical communication and improvisation skills, and have learned to think on our feet in accommodating changes and new dynamics. Adding a new instrument and musician to the mix is always a positive learning experience, not to mention the experience of further releasing and sharing a special, uniting musical energy.

Moving beyond the social aspect and looking at catharsis, there are moments in our music-making when an almost telepathic communication seems to transpire. Here, we make appropriate changes and musical gestures without any cues and seem to meet in the invisible nucleus of the music. This occurs most often when we're playing familiar songs, but also sneaks up and grabs us in the middle of a successful improvisation. This is best described in the band members' words. Dan said, "It's a high." Jim said, "It's a morgasm—a musical orgasm." Chris said, "There's a point in time when we had those grooves where we were literally telepathically speaking." Steve said, "It's the joy of creation." Dan said, "It's euphoria, dude!"

Every member of the group has expressed and been witnessed experiencing this catharsis through our music-making and group connection. In my second observation, I made a point of concentrating on non-verbal communication and actions that may give some insight into the personal experience. Dan makes his "bass face," which is a combination of concentration and pure joy. When Jim is in "the zone," he does a distinctive little dance while he plays guitar, closes his eyes, bangs his head, and bounces rhythmically. When Chris goes into his catharsis at the drums, his head tilts back, his eyes glaze over, and he relaxes into a beautiful peaceful smile. Steve's face contorts into an ear-to-ear Cheshire cat smile when he's in the moment on guitar. Michael dances, jumps, morphs expressions, and smiles during his catharsis on percussion. According to the other members, when I'm in that magical place, I give "great shut-eyed, nose-crinkled singer's face," I smile a lot, and I dance around without inhibition. In addition to the personal catharsis that occurs, there is a lot of eye contact, warm smiles, pointing in a gesture of acknowledging what the others are experiencing, and other actions indicative of us feeding off each other's energy.

Because work, school, and family are top priorities for the members of the band, time away from them is the main sacrifice we make to come to rehearsals. We experience morning-after consequences, as well. Steve said, "Going in early (to work) the next day is rough." I often feel tired. Dan and Chris agreed that they sacrifice brain cells and occasionally suffer hangovers. Dan said, "My wife does not understand this whole band culture thing." Michael has mentioned that his wife gives him grief for coming to rehearsals and when asked if Dan also deals with this, he said, "No, unless I come home inexcusably late or I'm hungover the next day. She doesn't like me doing harm to my body." Most members agreed that the sacrifices are worth it, however. Jim said, "I love making time for the music and I'll tell you what. I miss a Wednesday and I feel it…and boy, Thursday morning (after a rehearsal) I always wake up, it doesn't matter how tired I am, or anything, I just wake up with energy and I'm ready to go after a night of playing. It's a re-charge."

Stress relief, camaraderie, creativity, and improved musical skills are distinct benefits of music-making for SRB. These are the reasons why we fit band into our busy schedules. Beyond the obvious, however, are the benefits of socialization and catharsis.

The social dynamic of this group has unmistakably evolved into something exceptional. While most people have a circle of friends and various networks for socialization, very few have this kind of opportunity to connect and experience the SRB love and energy. This is truly a blessing for us and I don't know that it could be manufactured elsewhere. Anshel & Kipper (1988) suggested that the elicitation of trust and cooperation requires the type of involvement that combines both music and activity, such as group singing. As this applies to the current study, trust and cooperation are established and enhanced through group music-making in both performance and social contexts. Trust and cooperation are imperative for performing and can be achieved regardless of the social dynamic. With SRB, however, our social experience thrives within that cocoon of trust and cooperation and is further transcended into friendship. This would not change if we stopped making music together. Our friendships will thrive indefinitely.

The cathartic process of personal insight and self-actualization is one that we have individually enjoyed because of our group music-making experience. I feel incredibly fortunate to say that I better know and understand myself—and these other swell individuals—because of the catharsis created and sustained through music. It cannot be prescribed or directed. It can only be experienced, perhaps by serendipity, and I find this to be the greatest benefit of making time for band. Through our catharsis, the combined vibrations of our rejoicing human spirits can be seen and felt deep within.

The perceived benefits (and sacrifices) compared rather well among members of the band. Only one area emerged as another potential benefit, and that is the business angle. SRB's business involves completing a demo CD, structuring and finalizing original tunes, booking gigs, and generating revenue. We typically discuss business every few weeks, at the beginning of a rehearsal or during a break. These meetings are conducted with some resistance and trepidation, as nobody seems to want to manage that aspect of the band. We always have an agenda, but rarely reach our goals. It's not a big issue for the band, though, because making money isn't our top priority. Extra coin is nice, but we have agreed that we could never become a steady working band because of our other commitments. There was a point in time when a few of us wanted to work toward that, but we eventually accepted that it was not realistic without a concerted effort to boost discipline, an agent/manager, and a few more hours in the day. Some of us have felt frustrated by that lacking element in the band. Concern has been expressed that we're not going anywhere, yet we have so much potential. However, when we discuss ways to achieve our goals and attempt to assign various responsibilities to one another, nobody delegates, accepts, or follows up. We have agreed that even though we are progressing slowly, we have progressed, and we will always be open to outside management if and when that becomes a priority.

All members of the band have expressed that their involvement with the group is indefinite. Steve said, "We haven't been torn apart for various tensions or interpersonal reasons. That's something you could definitely claim as a success between us that we're still playing because our personalities all click." When asked what would make us walk away, responses included the studio burning down, death of a member, moving away, and extreme change in musical direction. It is highly unlikely that the members of SRB will go their separate ways anytime soon. *(Note: This study was conducted almost twenty years ago and it's safe to say that while some have migrated, we absolutely have NOT gone our separate ways!)*

To recap, busy professionals with full time work and family responsibilities make time for weekly music-making for a number of reasons. The experience provides stress relief, camaraderie, and an outlet for releasing creative energy. Musical techniques are experimented with and skills are improved. Sacrifices are minimal and worth making for the rewards.

The social aspect of SRB is one of the most important benefits. Beyond talking, partying, and laughing together at rehearsals, the group merges music into every social situation. We camp, boat, and hike together. We celebrate whatever, whenever, and music is always a uniting force.

The other important benefit of music-making together for SRB is the experience of catharsis. The joy and euphoria of connecting through music is felt through the energy of every individual. When combined, an ineffable unification and revelry are experienced.

Mary Hall, Artist

Rather astounding, music. I could go on and on with the empirical evidence of music's potential, but I think you get the general idea. As we segue from this chapter to the next, about music therapy, consider the holistic perspective of music as medicine in Christine Stevens' Hoop of Harmony (2012):

- Rhythm is medicine for the body
- Melody is medicine for the heart
- Harmony is medicine for the soul
- Silence is medicine for the mind
- Inner music is medicine for the spirit

# IV. RECAPITULATION

*"We're all feeling. Stop the bleeding. You're back to believing. Love is the answer and music is healing." —Florida Georgia Line*

If you listen to music to simply elevate your mood, you are using music therapeutically. The application of music for learning, developing, coping, and much more is music therapy at its core. Now that you have some related context in general music, let's delve into my heart and my calling…music therapy.

Modern music therapy began in the mid-1700s, when many physicians were also trained musicians who wrote about the use of music in medicine. Today, music therapy is a well-established profession, considered a behavioral science, and a diverse treatment modality (Crowe, 2004). Yes, again, I defer to music therapy guru and goddess, Barb Crowe's take on the evolution of music and healing.

Music had various uses in early human civilization. The following three roles of music relate to the history of music and healing. First, music is a key to knowledge of universal law. Music has always been a source of knowledge with its connection to mathematics, science, numbers, and mysticism. Second, music is a way to worship, interact with, placate, and engage the Divine. The link between music and religious worship is still prominent today. Third, music is a direct healing tool and support for general well-being. Throughout history, music has been used as a curative agent and a support to natural balance, harmony, and wellness. (Crowe, 2004)

Here is a brief timeline of music and healing:

## Music in Preliterate Cultures

- Music was often connected to supernatural forces—an ill person was seen as the victim of an evil spell or as a sinner against a tribal god. Medicine men utilized music to appease the gods who had caused the illness or to drive away evil spirits from one's body and/or mind.
- Drums, shakers, chants, and songs were used in healing ceremonies.

## Music in Early Civilization

- Music played a prominent role in rational medicine—the early study of health and disease based on empirical evidence.
- Music was used in magical and religious healing ceremonies.

## Music in Antiquity/Healing Rituals

- In ancient Greece, music was regarded as a special force over thought, emotion, and physical health; music was used to cure mental disorders.
- The study of health and disease was based on empirical evidence for the first time in history.
- People sang, danced, and played (crude) instruments to request rain and other survival needs from the heavens and supernatural forces.

## Music in the Middle Ages and Renaissance

- Christianity became a major force in Western civilization and influenced attitudes toward sick people, who were viewed as neither inferior nor being punished for their sins.
- Advances in anatomy, physiology, and clinical medicine marked the beginning of the scientific approach to medicine.
- Hospitals were established to provide humanitarian care to people with physical ailments, although the mentally ill population was mistreated.
- Music was used during the Renaissance as a remedy for melancholy, despair, and madness, but was also prescribed as preventive medicine; its potential as a tool for emotional health was recognized.

## Baroque Period

- Music to treat disease was closely linked with medical practice.
- Music started playing a role in the amelioration of mental disorders.
- It was believed that personality characteristics could be equated to specific types of music, making it necessary for the healer to strategically choose the appropriate musical style for treatment.

## Eighteenth Century

- Music was still popular in the treatment of disease, but a shift was underway to a more scientific approach to medicine.
- Accounts of music therapy in Europe and the United States first appeared as physicians, psychiatrists, and musicians supported its use in the treatment of physical and mental disorders.

- It was acknowledged that the skilled use of music in the treatment of disease requires a properly trained practitioner.

## Nineteenth Century

- Music therapy was used regularly in hospitals and other institutions, but almost always in conjunction with other therapies.
- Music was used to treat both mental and physical illness.
- Support was mounting for the use of therapeutic music as an alternative or supplement to traditional medicine.

## Early Twentieth Century

- Music therapy started gaining support among physicians, psychiatrists, and the general public.
- Music therapy was first formally practiced with WWII veterans to boost morale, treat "shell shock," and promote leisure skills, socialization, and physical and emotional functioning.
- Music therapy was being developed in educational settings; undergraduate and graduate curricula began during the mid-1940s.

## Later Twentieth Century

- Music therapy was acknowledged as an acceptable treatment modality with more populations being served.
- The National Association of Music Therapy (NAMT) formed in 1950; the American Association of Music Therapy (AAMT) was formed in 1971. The two merged to form the American Music Therapy Association (AMTA) in 1998.

## Twenty-first Century

- Music therapy is recognized as a strong, viable profession.

(Davis, Gfeller & Thaut, 1999)

Today, nearly 10,000 music therapists in the United States and abroad hold the Music Therapist-Board Certified (MT-BC) credential from the Certification Board for Music Therapists (CBMT), which is a sign of growing professional commitment to excellence (CBMT, 2021). Zippia (2021) reported the 2020 music therapist workforce in the US at 26,651 strong. The disparity in those numbers is likely attributed to those practicing without board-certification. To clarify, therapeutic music is not music therapy; however, some have been known to practice with expired certification or under the umbrella of therapeutic arts. (Please don't do that.) Zippia's number may also reflect support and ancillary positions in the music therapy arena.

Music therapists complete a rigorous education and training program, and earn a four-year bachelor's degree from an accredited university, which involves extensive training in all aspects of music. Students complete courses in clinical application of music, music theory, music history, music education, composition, performance, conducting, and research and analysis, as well as ancillary disciplines including anatomy/physiology, biology, physics, neuroscience, musicology, acoustics/psychoacoustics, human development, social and behavioral sciences, abnormal psychology, special education, anthropology, cultural/ethnic/gender/religious/spiritual traditions and considerations, and movement/dance.

Following coursework and pre-internship practicum experiences, a six-month full-time clinical internship (1,200 hours) is completed. Then the student must pass the board certification exam to hold the MT-BC credential. To maintain the credential, music therapists must complete one-hundred continuing education credits in five-year cycles. Many deepen their practice and/or pursue a career in academia with a master's or doctorate degree in music therapy.

Music and music therapy are part of integrative medicine and health. Music therapy is an evidence-based practice. Music therapists are part of the interdisciplinary team (doctors, nurses, social workers, physical therapists, occupational therapists, speech-language pathologists, chaplains, etc.).

A music therapist uses music within the context of a therapeutic relationship to elicit positive change in individuals developmentally, physically, intellectually, socially, emotionally/psychologically, existentially, and spiritually. Research has illustrated the relationship between music therapy and psychoneuroimmunology—the relationship between psychology, neurology, and immunology. (Cool word. Say it ten times fast.) With evidence-based music-infused strategies, we trained and credentialed music therapists can make a big difference.

So, what exactly *is* music therapy? Simply defined, music therapy is an ancillary healthcare profession using music as the foundation for therapeutic interaction. This is AMTA's official definition: "Music therapy means the clinical and evidence-based use of music interventions to accomplish individualized goals for people of all ages and ability levels within a therapeutic relationship by a credentialed professional who has completed an approved music therapy program. Music therapists develop music therapy treatment plans specific to the needs and strengths of the client who may be seen individually or in groups. Music therapy treatment plans are individualized for each client. The goals, objectives, and potential strategies of the music therapy services are appropriate for the client setting" (AMTA 2021).

Applied by a qualified practitioner, music therapy is the systematic use of music to achieve non-musical goals for a wide variety of clients and their families in numerous settings, including hospitals, physical and neurological rehabilitation facilities, medical clinics, centers for developmental disabilities, day treatment centers, group homes, mental/behavioral health agencies, drug and alcohol programs, general and state hospitals, geriatric care programs, assisted living facilities, hospices, public and private schools, special education programs, correctional facilities, residential facilities, research programs, private practices, and prevention and wellness programs.

## MUSIC THERAPY POPULATIONS FROM A-Z

Abused, attention deficit disorder (ADD), attention deficit/hyperactivity disorder (ADHD), aggression, acquired immunodeficiency syndrome (AIDS), Alzheimer's, anorexia, anxiety, at-risk youth, autism spectrum disorder (ASD)

Behavioral disorders, bipolar disorder, brain injuries, bulimia

Cancer, cerebral palsy, chemical dependency, chronic pain, comatose, communication disorders, chronic obstructive pulmonary disease (COPD)

Deaf, dementia, depression, developmental disabilities, down's syndrome

Early childhood, eating disorders, emotionally disturbed

Fluency of speech disorders, forensics

Geriatrics

Hard of hearing, head injury, hematology, human immunodeficiency virus (HIV), hospice, hospital

Immunology, impulse control disorders

Juvenile offenders

Kidney disease

Learning disabled, leukemia

Medical, mental health, multiply disabled

Neonatal care/neonatal intensive care unit (NICU), neurologically impaired

Obstetrics, oppositional defiance disorder (ODD)

**P**arkinson's disease, palliative care, physically disabled, prisoners, psychosis, post-traumatic stress disorder (PTSD)

**Q**uadriplegia

**R**ehabilitation, Rett syndrome

**S**chizoaffective disorder, schizophrenia, school-aged, sensory impairments, sex offenders, speech impairments, stroke, substance abuse, suicidal ideation, surgical

**T**erminally ill

**U**nipolar depression

**V**isually impaired

**W**ellness

**X**-linked disorders

**Y**outh at-risk

**Z**ieve's syndrome

Music therapy addresses all domains of human operations to help individuals attain and maintain maximum levels of functioning. Treatment involves strategic use of music, focused for healing, learning, and change. Examples of music interventions include singing, playing instruments, creative movement, receptive listening, music-based discussion, songwriting, drawing to music, musical games and stories, improvisation, sensory integration, and sound exploration.

Here is a more comprehensive list, alphabetical, mostly pilfered from AMTA:

- Active music making
- Chanting
- Composing
- Drawing to music

- Drumming
- Improvisation
- Instrument making
- Instrument playing
- Life review/reminiscence
- Lyric analysis
- Melodic Intonation Therapy (MIT)
- Movement to music/dance
- Music and imagery/Guided Imagery and Music (GIM)
- Music appreciation
- Music combined with other creative arts
- Music instruction
- Music performance
- Music skill building
- Music to reinforce behavior
- Musical games
- Musical stories
- Music-assisted cognitive reframing
- Music-based discussion
- Neurological interventions
- Pre-academic and academic skill building
- Progressive muscle relaxation
- Receptive music listening
- Rhythm and drumming
- Rhythmic Auditory Stimulation (RAS)
- Sensory integration
- Singing

- Social/recreational music
- Songwriting
- Sound exploration
- Sound vibration
- Toning/Humming (chakra work)
- Vibrotactile stimulation

> AMTA's Standards of Clinical Practice state that music therapists have an ethical responsibility to act in the best interest of the clients they serve to maximize their clients' potential and prognosis. If music therapy is not the most effective form of treatment for a client (or potential client), the therapist will refer that client to a more appropriate service (e.g., Occupational Therapy, Physical Therapy, Speech/Language Pathology, etc.).

The client's/patient's emotional state, past experiences, memories, social experiences, and previous exposure to music are all vital factors in the music therapy process (Crowe, 2004), although patients or clients need not possess any musical talent or experience to participate. Music is the springboard for therapeutic interaction because of its potential for health and learning. Here are some more impressive factoids related to music therapy:

## SOUND CONNECTIONS

- When listening to and participating in music, there is a positive chemical change in the brain as endorphins are released.
- Music therapy has been proven to improve respiration, lower blood pressure, improve cardiac output, reduce heart rate, and relax muscle tension.

- Music stimulates all the senses and involves individuals at many levels, which facilitates developmental skills.
- The link between music and brain function persists throughout adult life. Even when the brain stops growing, it never stops learning, and when injury strikes, music can help on the road to recovery.
- The brain processes music in both hemispheres and can therefore stimulate cognitive functioning and remediation of speech/language skills.

### Music can:

- improve cognitive skills (learning, perception, recognition, discrimination, categorization, memory, etc.)
- improve communication (receptive and expressive language skills)
- increase attention span/attention to task and alertness
- promote grounding
- reinforce pre-academic and academic skills (math, language/reading, etc.)
- increase motivation
- increase emotional awareness and promote appropriate emotional expression
- decrease inappropriate behaviors
- increase impulse control and frustration tolerance
- improve motor functioning and motor skills
- increase involvement and participation
- improve group behaviors (sharing, turn-taking, working in a group, etc.)

- improve self-esteem and provide a sense of accomplishment

Here are some sample music therapy goals, broken down by domain:

**Communication:** improve receptive language, expressive language, verbal communication, nonverbal communication

**Cognitive:** improve rational thinking, orientation to time, place and person, attention to task, attention to teacher, therapist, caregiver

**Educational:** improve pre-academic skills, academic skills

**Physical:** improve sensory-motor skills, sensory integration, perceptual-motor skills, proprioception, gross motor coordination, fine motor coordination, eye-hand coordination, adaptation to physical challenges, breath control, blood pressure, regular gait

**Psychosocial:** improve self-awareness, self-esteem, self-concept, awareness of environment, insight, adjustment, motivation, coping mechanisms, interpersonal interaction, family relationships, cooperation, compliance, self-discipline, impulse control

**Emotional:** improve expressivity, creativity, spontaneity, mood

**Self-Actualization:** improve self-realization, fulfillment, meaning, self-discovery

**Daily Living:** improve self-help (eating, toileting, bathing, dressing, etc.), independence

**Musical:** improve musical ability, musical potential, musical repertoire, freedom to express musically, peak musical experiences

**Leisure:** improve use of free time, leisure time options

**Vocational:** improve productivity, satisfaction

**Spiritual:** improve authenticity, presence

**Quality of Life:** improve well-being, personal growth, acceptance

(Hanser, 2018)

Considering age groups, music therapy for children can address communication, sensory needs, physical challenges, cognition, behaviors, communication, motor skills, self-awareness, social interaction, functional abilities and activities of daily living (ADLs), self-expression, self-esteem, and emotional identification and appropriate expression. Music therapy with adolescents typically has more of an emotional/behavioral focus. Music therapy for adults may address medical conditions, mental health issues, corrections/forensics, neurologic rehabilitation, community music therapy, and health and wellness. Music therapy with older adults often addresses end of life issues.

The music therapy treatment process involves referral, assessment, treatment planning and implementation, documentation and evaluation, and ultimately, termination of services. Relationships may be as few as one visit to years-long, depending on the needs and goals of the client or patient.

I'm going to get a little research-y here and share highlights from formal pieces I wrote about 1) music and emotions, 2) music therapy with depression, and 3) music-as-therapy to avoid burnout in the profession (perceptions from board-certified music therapists). I hope you gain further insight into the potential and power of music therapy from a behavioral science perspective.

## MUSIC AND EMOTIONS

Music is important to human beings largely because we find it personally relevant. We respond emotionally to music in a number of ways. *Affective response* to music involves emotions, feelings, and moods. Typically, "happy" music is major with ascending melodies, upbeat, and high-pitched, while "sad" music is minor with descending melodies, slow, and low-pitched. Harmonies, when consonant, are heard as serene and lyrical. Dissonance may create excitement and suspense; however, too much may cause agitation.

*Physiological responses* to music include changes in heart rate, respiration, and galvanic skin response (GSR). Generally speaking, stimulative music, characterized by strong and familiar melodies, driving rhythms, and intense volumes, enhances energy and emotion. Sedative music, characterized by sustained melodies, weaker legato rhythms, and softer volumes, evokes physical calm.

*Learned behavior response* relates to experience, expectation, repetition, and culture. Research suggests that music must be familiar to elicit an emotional response. Humans have developed expectations regarding what will come next in music. When expectations are met, one experiences pleasure. When expectations are violated, one experiences anxiety. Deep satisfaction comes with deviation of anticipation when it sets up a stronger resolution. Emotional response to music is a subject of broad consideration, and a large body of research supports their connection.

It is clear from several studies that music can affect a variety of behaviors including anxiety, symbolic sexual arousal, interpersonal interactions, self-concept, and test performance. There is also ample evidence that music can produce physiological effects, which, in turn, affect human emotions. The physiological experience of an emotion is accompanied by various physiological changes. Barely escaping a car collision leaves one with a pounding heart, sweaty palms, and rapid breathing. Lie detector tests demonstrate how physiological processes accompany emotion, as they measure various physiological processes, which are assumed to change with emotional upset.

The mechanisms that control and shape affective responses go beyond musical structure. They encompass the central nervous system, periodicity, oscillations and other aspects of timing, the limbic system, frontal lobes, and sensory cortex. Stimulative music, which enhances energy and emotions by affecting the striped muscles and subcortical reactors, is characterized by such elements as strong rhythms, loud volume, and a disjunctive melodic line. Sedative music, which tends to evoke physical calm and intellectual, contemplative behaviors, is characterized by a more sustained and conjunct melodic nature, with strong rhythms and percussive elements largely lacking.

The majority of results drawn from the literature suggest the following: 1) Stimulative music tends to increase heart rate or pulse rate, while sedative music tends to cause a decrease. 2) Blood pressure does vary in music listening situations. 3) Stimulative music tends to increase respiration and sedative music tends to decrease it. 4) Stimulative and sedative music produce different effects on GSR; however, most commonly, stimulative music produces greater GSR deflections than sedative music. Various elements of music, such as pitch range, melody, and rhythm affect GSR readings. 5) Stimulative music increases muscular activity as recorded through electromyography (EMG) and through observation of bodily activity. Specific emotions, such as hate, grief, or joy, caused by music listening produce distinct, differential muscle movements in the fingertips. Stimulative music causes papillary dilation and sedative music causes stronger peristaltic (stomach) contractions than stimulative music. 6) Musicians produce more alpha brain waves than non-musicians during music listening situations. Children spend more time in alpha brain wave production during silence than during any of several aural conditions. Electroencephalography (EEG) was used here to measure response to music.

Many terms and concepts coincide with that of learned behavior, including conditioning, culture, experience, expectation, repetition, memory, and training. Expectation and familiarity are the most attributed aspects of learned behavior in emotional responses to music. These mood responses are essentially determined by one's previous experience with music. It has been suggested that musically evoked reactions are not feelings, but memories of feelings. This explains how one piece of music can cause markedly different reactions among different listeners. Learned behavior is a strong determinant of emotional response to music. Expectation/familiarity, repetition, memory, and training are the predominant factors in conditioning, which translate into emotional response.

(Abeles, 1980; Biller, Olson & Green, 1974; Boltz, 1998; Epstein, 1993; Goins, 1998; Haack, 1980; Higgins, 1997; Hodges, 1980; Jourdain, 1997; Levinson, 1997; Noy, 1993; Ostwald, 1966; Radocy & Boyle, 1988; Rose, 1993; Stratton & Zalanowski, 1997; Walton, 1997; Zimney, 1961)

With such a strong connection between music and emotions, music therapy can be a highly effective intervention for various behavioral health disorders. Next, I'm going to home in specifically on depression. The United States, with all its wealth and progress and glory, is one of the most depressed countries in the world. Symptoms of an anxiety or depressive disorder continue to increase as mental health care needs go unmet.

## MUSIC THERAPY AND ADULTS WITH DEPRESSION

Depression, otherwise known as Major Depressive Disorder or Clinical Depression, is a common and serious mood disorder, as described in the American Psychiatric Association's *Diagnostic and Statistical Manual of Mental Disorders*. Those who suffer from it experience persistent feelings of sadness and hopelessness. They lose interest in activities they once enjoyed. Additional symptoms include chronic pain, digestive issues, significant weight loss or weight gain, loss of energy, fatigue, feelings of worthlessness or guilt, difficulty concentrating, indecisiveness, and suicidal ideation (APA, 2021).

Depression is one of many emotional disorders for which music therapy can change behaviors and patterns of thinking, making a positive difference in the client's ability to function in everyday life. Clinical uses of music therapy in the psychiatric setting vary as greatly as the clientele. Because music is so flexible and appealing, it has great potential as a treatment tool with widely diverse therapeutic functions.

Common goals of music therapy for this population include improving self-esteem and self-image, increasing emotional awareness, improving emotional expression, combating isolation and withdrawal, improving coping skills, improving volition and motivation, promoting a sense of hope, increasing attention span, establishing and/or improving interpersonal relationships, improving group behaviors, promoting a sense of belonging, and improving gross motor movement and physical activity.

Group therapy is often preferred over 1:1 therapy with depressed adults because of its many benefits of social interaction. One advantage to being in a group for psychiatric treatment (including music therapy treatment) is that clients realize their problems are not unique and the environment provides a safe, supportive setting to share emotional insights and practice interpersonal skills.

Specific music therapy activity interventions for depressed adults include singing, reminiscence, issue-based songwriting, lyric analysis, improvisation, rhythmic movement, composing and playing music, and listening and responding to music. While familiar songs are beneficial for singing, unknown songs may be used in a group therapy environment to induce emotional response and encourage discussion.

The following are possible interactions between music and words in therapy: 1) When the emotional material is too painful to bear, the musical framework may support the patient and help ventilate the overloaded content. 2) Interaction between music and words in a song form may characterize the opening and closing of sessions. 3) When patients encounter difficulty continuing with a session and need relief, music may facilitate relaxation and pave the way toward verbal elaboration. 4) Music may serve as a container when the patient and therapist sustain an improvised sung dialogue or when the patient improvises a monologue that requires accompaniment. 5) In role-playing or storytelling, music represents and symbolizes objects, key figures, etc., and may enhance the process of working through issues. 6) The most open technique is free singing of associations without musical support from the therapist, usually done in a style of incantation or recitation (Wigram & DeBacker, 1999).

Because music is an emotional language that elicits thoughts and feelings, it can be a powerful tool for increasing emotional expression and self-awareness. Listening and responding to music can use that emotional language to help clients become more aware of their feelings and thoughts, while promoting discussion, social interaction, and personal insight, and even motivating desirable behavioral changes. A client may relive feelings of anxiety through a musical listening experience, for example. The therapist helps the client reflect on those feelings and make connections between the feelings experienced in the session and real-life situations. The client, with the therapist's guidance, can then begin to formulate concrete plans for therapeutic change (Davis, Gfeller & Thaut, 1999).

The third piece I'd like to share with you in this chapter is from my thesis for my Master of Music in Music Therapy degree, published in 2013. When I landed on this topic for my study, "self-care" had become a big buzzword. At the time, I explored this from a professional music therapists' perspective. Reviewing it now, nine years later, I see parallels to the non-music therapist as far as using music for personal therapy. As you read the next few pages, bear in mind how this content might apply to you.

## A SURVEY OF BOARD-CERTIFIED MUSIC THERAPISTS: THE IMPACT OF STRESS AND BURNOUT, AND THE NEED FOR SELF-CARE

ABSTRACT: This mixed-method, descriptive research study involved an 800+ person survey of board-certified music therapists about the impact of stress and burnout in the profession and the need for self-care. Respondents identified healthy diet and rest as primary activities of self-care, followed by recreation/leisure time with loved ones, exercise, hobbies, and prayer. Music therapists reportedly continue to feel motivated and inspired in the profession predominantly because of the gratification/satisfaction of the results of their work, followed by engagement in self-care, loving the work regardless of income, attending conferences and symposiums, diversification among various populations, and keeping professional life separate from personal life. ANOVA results indicated that job satisfaction and engagement in self-care likely increase with age; job satisfaction is higher among married music therapists, those with children, and those with more than thirty years in practice; and those with no children and those with a master's or doctorate degree are more likely to engage in self-care.

The music therapy profession, one of many helping professions, is both highly rewarding and meaningful, and emotionally and physically draining. Many music therapists experience a high level of stress on the job due to the emotionally charged nature of the work and the potential for physical exhaustion. Most people are inundated with media coverage of school violence, terrorism, and general ugliness in the world. Personal losses, family conflicts, uncertainty in the workplace, among other things, contribute to an individual's stress, anxiety, and general outlook. To counter the effects of stress, music therapists need to practice self-care. This study was undertaken to determine what percentage of therapists engage in self-care and which techniques are most utilized.

The music therapist's work environment involves daily exposure to what I call the devastating Ds: disease, disability, disfigurement, dysfunction, disaster, even death. Music therapists must constantly think on their feet for their clients, often feeling exposed and suffocated. We witness families grieving, clients struggling, and policies impeding advancement. We regularly observe people in physical and emotional pain, dealing with stunted functioning and the need for conflict resolution. It's not always pretty. To a music therapist, all of this can be downright depressing, discouraging, depleting, desensitizing, deflating, and destructive.

Despite all this, we remain optimistic and passionate about music therapy. We celebrate our clients' baby steps of progress and breakthroughs. We continue to establish long-term goals and behavioral objectives designed for success, learning, and healing. It seems to be in a music therapist's nature to be flexible and resilient. The positive outlook that is inherent in this line of work may balance some of the drawbacks, but the inconsistency and other negative aspects of the profession can take its toll on a music therapist's attitude and motivation.

The topic of this research became somewhat of a personal crusade for this author, as I myself had fallen victim to the overwhelming demands of the profession and my own tendency to take on too much. While in graduate school, I was working full time between three jobs and managing a family. Complexity science tells us that we're healthiest on the edge of chaos (Crowe, 2004), yet I found myself spiraling into the chaos! I had no time whatsoever to engage in self-care. I was sleep-deprived, stressed out, and burned out for longer than I care to admit. My vocal health was being compromised, my physical and emotional health were being adversely affected, and my personal relationships were falling into disrepair as a result. As a conscious effort in self-care, I sought professional counseling and started developing strategies to reprioritize, simplify, and slow down. But that's easier said than done. Over-functioning just seems to be in my nature and apparently, I'm not alone.

As I began this investigation into the phenomenon of professional burnout and need for self-care, I discovered that many of my colleagues were in a similar situation. I realized that we need to get a handle on all of this not only for our own wellness, but so that we can be mindful and fully present with and for our clients. Music therapists give so much of themselves through sympathy, empathy, and treatment. There's a certain degree of drive and control in a helping professional's personality that might become an overdeveloped sense of responsibility. We are champions for our clients, but what about for ourselves? Here's a little background.

Occupational burnout is a growing problem among helping professionals who work in human services, such as music therapy, occupational therapy, physical therapy, speech/language pathology, psychology, social work, nursing, caregiving, and teaching. The online *Merriam-Webster Dictionary* (2013) defined burnout as, "exhaustion of physical or emotional strength or motivation, usually as a result of prolonged stress or frustration." According to Freudenberger (1974), "occupational stress" or "burnout" is to "fail, wear out, or become exhausted by making excessive demands on energy, strength, or resources." Cherniss (1980) described burnout as, "a process that begins with excessive and prolonged levels of job stress. The process is completed when workers defensively cope with the job stress by psychologically detaching themselves from the job and becoming apathetic, cynical, or rigid."

Burnout occurs over time and may develop in a series of five stages: honeymoon, fuel shortage, chronic symptoms, crisis, and hitting the wall (Greenberg, 2002). Individuals feel high levels of job satisfaction in the honeymoon stage. During the fuel shortage stage, individuals begin to fatigue and have difficulty sleeping, which may lead to the chronic symptoms stage of exhaustion, susceptibility to disease, and the psychological effects of anger and depression. In the crisis stage, the individual can develop an illness that may result in loss of work and personal relationship challenges. Symptoms of the final stage, hitting the wall, can contribute to life-threatening illnesses such as heart disease or cancer.

Stress affects everyone, yet different people experience different stressors. The response of the body to change, demand, pressure, or threat from outside is known as the stress response. The aim of the stress response is to bring the agitated body back to normal and enable it to protect itself from the external situation. Excessive stress can cause physical, psychological, emotional, and social damage. Ideal stress management involves finding one's own optimal level of stress for healthy functioning (Cotton, 1990; Jaffe & Scott, 1984).

Rowe (1999) described how some individuals may be more prone to stress and burnout due to a lack of "cognitive hardiness." She said "hardy" individuals view life with interest and excitement and demonstrate characteristics of control, commitment, and challenge. A "high hardy" individual will perceive a stressful event in a more positive light and will be less likely to perceive it as a stressor. Rush (1995) found that high hardy individuals utilize control coping—proactive coping and cognitive assessments of the situation. "Low hardy" individuals are more likely to engage in escape coping or avoidance of the stressor, which may result in built up stress and tension.

In a presidential column to members of the National Association for Music Therapy, Bitcom (1981) reported several factors that may contribute to burnout among music therapists, including constant change and adaptation to the point of apathy, overpolicing, unrealistic workloads with low pay, compromising ideals, lack of respect, continuous crisis intervention, "going by the book" leadership attitudes, limited opportunities for sharing and contributing to decision-making, and excessive control of emotional expression.

Overall, reasons cited for burnout among music therapists included unrealistic workloads, insufficient pay, limited job market, limited opportunities for advancement, making continuous adjustments due to crisis intervention, lack of administrative support, lack of respect and direction, compromising ideals, having to perform activities outside the field, micro management, lack of autonomy, lack of staff recognition, absence of adequate support networks or outside interests, boredom or lack of motivation, and problems or pressures in personal life (Bitcom, 1981; Knoll, Reuer, & Henry, 1988; Oppenheim, 1987).

Salmon and Stewart (2005) reported data from a survey of music therapists working with terminally ill patients and the stressors associated with this population. Continuous exposure to grief and death was the most cited source of stress. The manifestations of stress most identified were fatigue, feelings of inadequacy, sadness, illness, and avoidance of patients. Perceived related symptoms included fatigue, anxiety, lack of sleep, irritability, headache, depression, and muscle tension.

Additional job stressors reported in the literature include time constraints, conflict with co-workers and administration, and population-specific challenges. Other physical symptoms of burnout have been reported to include anxiety, exhaustion, increased use of drugs and alcohol, nervousness, insomnia, backaches, and headaches (Maher, 1983; Spicuzza & Devoe, 1982).

Closely related to stress and burnout is "compassion fatigue," a compelling condition that is characterized by physical and psychological exhaustion resulting from excessive professional demands that drain personal resources (Leon, Altholz & Dziegielewski, 1999). Compassion fatigue is often referred to as the cost of caring for people with emotional pain, and its detrimental effects can include exhaustion, an inability to focus, a decrease in productivity, unhappiness, self-doubt, and loss of passion and enthusiasm (Lester, 2010).

While compassion fatigue manifests itself differently in each individual, some common characteristics of compassion fatigue include decreased concern for clients, decrease in positive feelings or empathy for clients, physical and emotional exhaustion, increased job dissatisfaction, and feelings of hopelessness related to the job that carry over into other areas of the individual's life (Figley, 1995; Maslach, 1976; Pines & Kafry, 1978; Valent, 1995).

The concept of compassion fatigue has been linked to the potential development of what is commonly known today as secondary traumatic stress disorder (Figley, 1995). Figley identified causes of trauma in workers as 1) the use of empathy by the worker, 2) the worker's own traumatic experiences, 3) the resurfacing of the worker's unresolved trauma created by the victim's trauma, and 4) working with vulnerable populations such as traumatized children.

Because of the potential for and the detrimental consequences of stress and burnout, self-care is an absolute necessity for music therapists. Salmon and Stewart (2005) reported data from a national survey investigating self-care for the music therapy professional, evaluating the awareness of self-care needs and identifying the range of music experiences used to meet those needs. Ninety-five percent of participants reported using music outside of the workplace. Outside uses of music included listening to music, going to concerts, playing in a band, composing/ songwriting, performing, playing/singing for self, community/social music-sharing, and singing in a choral group. Outside music was reported to provide the benefits of supporting general coping, enhancing relaxation, energizing, releasing stress, providing an emotional outlet, facilitating self-expression, providing distraction, and stabilizing or centering the individual. Norman (2009) also found that music therapists who participate in music experiences more often have higher levels of work engagement, with some variation depending on type of experience, setting, and purpose.

Salmon and Stewart also reported areas of general support for self-care, which include family, friends, exercise, church, and leisure activities. The coping strategies most frequently identified were creative expression, spiritual practice, exercise, collegial support, and a social life outside of work. Many respondents who work in end-of-life care acknowledged their work as challenging and emotionally difficult, as well as rewarding, meaningful, and a privilege.

Professional or peer supervision is frequently mentioned in the literature as a means of professional self-care. Forinash (2001) said supervision is a journey, or odyssey of sorts, in which supervisor and supervisee learn and grow and from which both, very likely, leave transformed in some way. "While personal growth is not the focus of supervision, it is a common by-product for both participants."

Bitcom (1981) also suggested keeping in touch with other professionals through conferences or support groups, as well as other practical strategies including partaking in enjoyable extracurricular or recreational activities, eliminating unnecessary stress such as extra paperwork, developing and documenting personal goals, prioritizing family and friends, continuing education, being included in the employer's decision and policy making, and having a sense of humor.

In response to open-ended questions about personal coping strategies for reducing stress, Fowler (2006) found that respondents play music for fun, go to movies, read, scrapbook, get outdoors, exercise, get adequate rest, eat nutritiously, confide in coworkers and trusted friends, attend conferences, pray, leave work at the office, focus on the good things, and repeat the mantra, "It's not my problem."

Oppenheim (1987) suggested preventive measures to burnout, which include professional counseling, in-service training in health, nutrition, and stress management, daily exercise, hobbies, plenty of sleep, continued learning, maintaining unscheduled leisure hours, termination of unhealthy relationships, goal setting, and peer support.

Swezey (2013) stated that self-care can be seen as not only critical for individual professionals, but also for the growth of helping professions and the quality of care which clients receive. Swezey found the five most commonly used strategies for career sustaining behaviors to be the following: 1) maintain a sense of humor; 2) spend time with partner and/or family; 3) maintain self-awareness; 4) try to maintain objectivity about clients; and 5) reflect on positive experiences. A portion of the music therapy field was identified in his study as being at risk for burnout and secondary traumatic stress, both of which can affect satisfaction and client care. Swezey recommended that music therapy professionals take the time to assess the stressors of their work and the strategies they utilize for their professional well-being. He added that it is important for music therapists to use strategies in a variety of self-care domains, including psychological, physical, and spiritual.

Music therapists are more emotionally exhausted, feel less detached from their clients, and feel more confident and successful than the average mental health worker (Vega, 2010). Because music therapy is a distinctive and customizable profession, the music therapist's methods of self-care should be equally distinctive and customized.

*Phew! That's a lot of evidence for prioritizing our own needs, wouldn't you say? Results of the study follow. I omitted the methods and statistical gobbledygook that would send your eyeballs back into your skull. Again, consider any connections between these self-care findings and your world.*

Respondents of the study reportedly engage in a variety of self-care activities. Using Likert scale options of never, occasionally, monthly, weekly, and daily, respondents identified healthy diet and rest as primary activities of self-care, followed consecutively by recreation/leisure time with loved ones, exercise, hobbies, and prayer. Complete results appear in the following chart and table.

I participate in the following activities of self-care, outside of my music therapy practice:

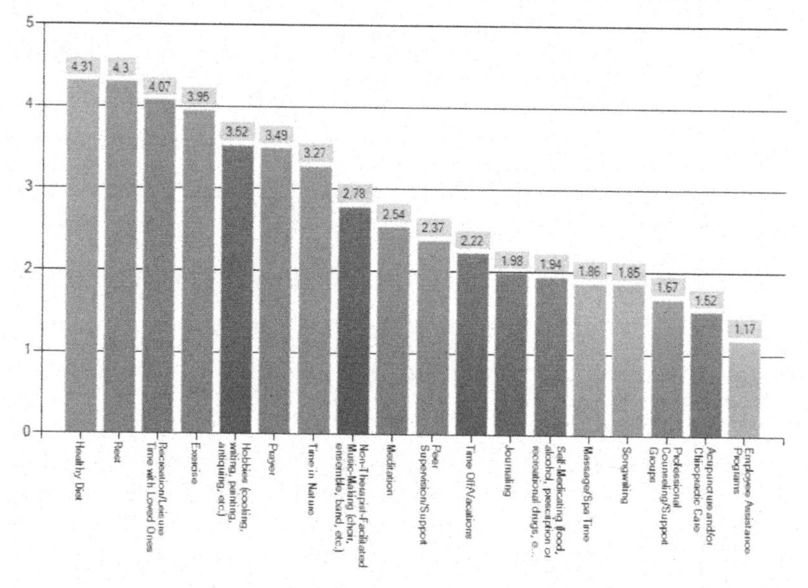

*Activities of Self-Care*

| Activity | Never | Occasionally | Monthly | Weekly | Daily |
|---|---|---|---|---|---|
| Healthy diet | 0.76% | 10.25% | 4.05% | 27.22% | 57.72% |
| Rest | 0.64% | 11.72% | 2.80% | 26.50% | 58.34% |
| Recreation/leisure time with loved ones | 0.63% | 6.84% | 8.10% | 53.80% | 30.63% |
| Exercise | 1.91% | 14.25% | 6.11% | 42.62% | 35.11% |
| Hobbies (cooking, writing, painting, antiquing, etc.) | 5.33% | 18.53% | 13.71% | 43.91% | 18.53% |
| Prayer | 19.39% | 17.22% | 1.91% | 17.86% | 43.62% |
| Time in Nature | 3.81% | 25.25% | 22.46% | 37.06% | 11.42% |
| Non-therapist-facilitated music-making (choir, ensemble, band, etc.) | 17.41% | 31.64% | 10.55% | 35.96% | 4.45% |
| Meditation | 32.19% | 29.26% | 4.33% | 20.99% | 13.23% |
| Peer supervision/support | 21.63% | 40.97% | 20.10% | 13.87% | 3.44% |
| Time off/vacations | 4.33% | 75.32% | 15.78% | 3.69% | 0.89% |
| Journaling | 42.09% | 36.48% | 7.78% | 8.93% | 4.72% |
| Self-medicating with food, alcohol, prescription or recreational drugs, etc. | 47.81% | 30.08% | 6.68% | 10.80% | 4.63% |
| Massage/spa time | 35.62% | 46.31% | 15.52% | 1.78% | 0.76% |
| Songwriting | 40.20% | 44.27% | 8.27% | 4.71% | 2.54% |
| Professional counseling/ support groups | 57.83% | 25.73% | 8.66% | 7.13% | 0.64% |
| Acupuncture and/or chiropractic care | 67.98% | 17.35% | 9.95% | 4.59% | 0.13% |
| Employee assistance programs | 88.57% | 11.98% | 2.06% | 0.26% | 0.13% |

An "Other" category permitted respondents to write in additional activities of self-care, which included the following:

- crying for release
- silence
- non-music/talk/comedy radio in the car before, between, and after sessions
- taking full hour lunch breaks
- personal acceptance
- reflecting on positive client reactions (e.g., smiles, hugs, progress, asking when the next session is, etc.)
- clinical supervision
- attending special trainings
- personal psychotherapy
- music improvisation/guided imagery/mandalas
- attending concerts
- listening to music
- learning a new instrument
- participating in peer groups (e.g., book clubs)
- yoga
- fostering animals
- shopping
- social media

The final question of the survey asked if participants have any experiences or insights about the need for music therapists to engage in self-care. Common themes from responses suggested the following:

- taking time for self
- separation/balance between work and home

- peer support and supervision
- personal therapy
- music-making outside of work
- non-musical hobbies
- exercise and nutrition
- vocal health
- spiritual practice
- meditation and reflection
- self-awareness/identity/ability to identify stressors
- population variety
- flexibility/willingness to make a change
- boundaries
- professional goals

We rationalize our lack of time for self-care but must learn to trust ourselves and the power of intention and nurture ourselves with the gift of proactive good health. We need to embrace our inner wisdom, as well as our inner child, and energize the inner spirit in the face of cynicism and over-functioning that has become the norm. Music therapists do not have to settle for feeling defeated and downtrodden. While the possibility of burnout is strong, it is not inevitable. With proper identification of triggers for stress/burnout and coping strategies through self-care, music therapists can remain active, motivated, inspired, challenged, and satisfied in the profession.

In conclusion, here are some pertinent quotes from the qualitative data gathered through the survey: experiences and perspectives about the need for music therapists to engage in self-care, specifically related to making music outside of work.

- "We are artists and need time to make our own art."

- "I try to use outside music making as often as possible. I believe for many music therapists, music is a powerful stress reliever, but there must be a musical outlet outside of work (the stressor)."
- "I am paid to play in a symphony on a regular basis and my symphony job is just as important to me as my music therapy job. Without an outlet for my own personal music making, it is hard for me to enjoy using music to help others."
- "If involvement in music-making is only done at work, music may become only a means of income—a music therapist may lose his/her true love for it."
- "I think it is very important to separate who you are as a musician and who you are as a music therapist. Often these get intertwined because it is our love and passion for music that led most of us to choose a career of music therapy. However, as a musician I need opportunities to create music and perform by myself and with other musicians. These opportunities cannot and should not be found within the music therapy sessions (ethics!). They must be found outside and away from music therapy."
- "For me, it was important to start making music for myself again. Music, which has been a huge part of my personal identity, had become something for my patients and when I started to perform and write songs again in my spare time, I became a more effective, happier, and healthier clinician. It was easier for me to be present with my patients and find meaning in the work."
- "I play piano at home on a regular basis for self-care because it's not an instrument I use regularly in sessions."
- "Playing in my own bands is what keeps me the most healthy."

I recently reflected on a lot of the research I conducted as a grad student and through my work on the ASU School of Music faculty. I am recognizing more and more every day how music functions in our lives, musicians or not. I encourage many of the aforementioned methods of self-care with my clients/patients today. Hobbies and recreational/leisure interests make highly effective coping strategies for emotional management and self-regulation.

Now that you hopefully have a solid grasp on the basics of music history, psychoneuroimmunological benefits of music, and music therapy, let's transition into the "TEMPO" portion of the book. How do music and lyrics tell the stories of our lives? A memory? A relationship? A tradition? More likely than not, there's a song for that.

# V. TEMPO

*"Walk on, walk on, with hope in your heart and you'll never walk alone."*
*—Rodgers & Hammerstein*

Let me give you a little back story on how the idea for this section of the book materialized. I had been mulling over a writing project about my experiences as a music therapist for some time but hadn't yet formulated any sort of game plan. I booked an overdue massage, which is way up there on my list of self-care essentials. I was getting my reflexology on when my mind began to wander. Imagine that. A quiet, relaxing, stress-sucking environment to tune out and go blank. Not me. I am incapable of quieting my mind and have ironically discovered peace in noise. Drumming, specifically (more on that ahead). Yet I was surrounded by nothing but quiet. My wheels were turning. They never stop. This time was different though. A low-frequency thrumming. Neurons firing. Cerebral twerking. Images of letters forming in my brain. The letters were M-O-P-E-T. They kept flittering around my closed eyelids until I memorized them. A post-massage puddle of goo, I grabbed my phone and searched "MOPET anagram" on Google. In addition to a few other legit words, the anagram spelled TEMPO! A sign? A message? Hells, yes. TEMPO became an acronym, a synaptic seed, which blossomed into the next five chapters of personal and clinical experiences about songs for that Tradition, Emotion, Memory, Person, and Occasion.

First, let's talk about tempo and how it relates to our daily existence. I mentioned in Chapter 2 that rhythm is a pattern of time, a recurring movement of sound, the relationship of tones over time. It involves duration, beat, meter, accent, and tempo. Here's a quick breakdown.

*Duration* is the length of time or how long or short a note or pitch is sounded. For example, a quarter note sounds for four beats. A half note is two beats. And so on. *Beat* is the basic unit of time, the pulse. It is the rhythm you tap your foot to when listening to music. *Meter* is a rhythmic pattern or grouping of temporal units (beats) into regular measures or bars. For example, 3/4 meter has three quarter note beats per measure. *Accent* is an emphasis on a particular note or set of notes, contributing to the articulation and ornamentation of musical phrases within a piece. The accented note pops in the texture. *Tempo* is the speed or pace of a piece of music. It is indicated at the start of a written piece, measured in beats per minute, and demonstrated by a conductor leading into performance. (A metronome is a blessing for practicing a piece and maintaining tempo.)

Consider each of these elements in your universe. Everything has duration, from your dairy products to the remaining days of the people you surround yourself with. Our routines are measured by scheduled durations…school and work, meals, events on our social calendars, napportunities (yes, I coined that one).

We all have our own beat. Some of us keep it slow and flowing (legato). Some are more articulated or even detached (staccato). Some march to a different beat (which is far more fun). We respond to beats in nature, produced sounds, and our own body percussion. Certainly you're guilty of drumming on the steering wheel with the volume cranked. I catch myself moving to beats all around me. I had a hospice patient years ago who had a Jack Russell terrier. The dog bounced to the beat of every song I sang, matching every tempo. It was hilarious. And remarkable.

Meter can be equated to the patterns in our lives, not necessarily sounded. Our internal meter is our heartbeat, pulse, and respiration. Musical meter can inspire a mood, from a gentle waltz to a raucous line dance. Meter is also related to mathematical systems that make us feel smart. I am a much better baker because I understand meter.

We have invisible accents all over our stories—traditions, emotions, memories, people, occasions! Think of those accents as parentheses for moments in your life. Are there patterns? Surprises? Highs? Lows?

Just as we have our own beat, we have our own tempo. The speed at which we work, play, and rest vary. Nobody moves at the same tempo all day, just as nobody feels the same emotion all day. Tempo is mutable, impressionable, and expressive, as are humans.

Just about everything we do can be related to music. We are creatures of rhythm. With a little bit of knowledge and intention, we can use rhythm for positive change in our lives. A perfect illustration of this is drumming for wellness.

Have you experienced drumming? A drum circle, for example, is a jam session with as few as two and as many as hundreds of participants. Drum circles are used for many purposes, including corporate team building, empowerment, spirit building, synergizing and rhythm training, stress and anger release, bonding, and community building. The goal is not precision or perfection, but is built on cooperation in the groove, using rhythm to unite people and celebrate life. Drummers synchronize their heartbeats, experiencing a rhythmic massage and emotional release. It is an energy-charged event that is both enjoyable and therapeutic for stress, bereavement, wellness, recreation, and expression.

## Benefits of Drumming:

- Strengthens the immune system—gets the heart pounding and blood pumping
- Releases endorphins, enhancing the brain's pleasure centers
- Enhances theta-wave production and brain wave synchronization
- Produces deeper self-awareness by inducing synchronous brain activity and promoting alpha waves; activates both sides of the brain and can help the mind achieve hemispheric coordination
- Re-establishes balance in opioid and serotonergic systems
- Increases DHEA-to-cortisol ratios, NK cell activity, and LAK cell activity
- Attenuates and/or reverses specific neuroendocrine and neuroimmune patterns of modulation associated with the classic stress response
- Produces cumulative or sustaining neuroendocrine or immunological effects that contribute to well-being
- Reverses stress on the genomic level
- Grounds a person into the body and the present moment
- Improves mood states and reduces burnout
- Offers creative expression
- Promotes emotional insight and release
- Provides a context for communication, especially with issues of anger, fear, guilt, denial, depression, and loneliness
- Promotes healing of emotional trauma, forgiveness, and release of guilt
- Reduces feelings of alienation and isolation
- Increases self-awareness and self-esteem
- Promotes self-assessment and self-realization

- Provides reinforcement and empowerment for personal change
- Increases alteration of consciousness and experiences of transcendence
- Promotes spiritual awakening and greater awareness of unconscious powers
- Provides a connection with others, community healing, bonding, and trust
- Provides an experience of camaraderie, group acceptance, and unity

Drumming is the equivalent of a full brain workout! It engages nearly every part of the brain at once:

- Frontal Lobe (the executive system—behavior, movement, cognitive flexibility, emotional regulation, personality, planning, decision making, and abstract thinking)
- Temporal Lobe (auditory processing, processing memory and meaning, visual memory retention, and comprehension of language)
- Brain Stem (basic vital body functions, breathing, heart rate, blood pressure, and digestion)
- Parietal Lobe (sensory information integration, processing bodily sensations, and processing language)
- Occipital Lobe (visual processing)
- Cerebellum (motor control, balance, coordination, posture, and motor learning)

(NeuroDrumming.com, 2021)

Drumming is a method of music-making that is truly for everyone. It does not require advanced physical abilities or specialized training. I encourage you to make drumming part of your personal prescription for wellness. More on that and other music-as-therapy for yourself in Chapter 11. I now invite you to enjoy a variety of personal and professional stories from my musical world, where's there's a song for that tradition, emotion, memory, person, and occasion.

# VI. THERE'S A SONG FOR THAT TRADITION

*"I see trees of green, red roses too. I see them bloom for me and you. And I think to myself, what a wonderful world." —Louis Armstrong*

Traditions are elements of culture, society, religion, and family, which are transmitted from one generation to the next. Traditions create a sense of belonging and provide stability through common experiences. While some traditions are centuries old and generally change very little with each generation, people may also establish new traditions in hopes that they will carry on.

A tradition might be as simple as Taco Tuesday with the family or Friday happy hour with the work gang. It can also be as extravagant as a private indigenous ceremony. Following is a list of common traditions:

- Authority
- Beliefs
- Conventions
- Craft
- Culture

- Daily connections
- Economy
- Etiquette
- Food
- Game night
- Identity
- Knowledge
- Language
- Lifestyle
- Military
- Music
- Norms
- Pastimes
- Rites of passage
- Rituals (baptism/immersion in water)
- Roles (family, age, gender, etc.)
- Rules
- Saturday brunch
- Social systems
- Storytelling/myth
- Values
- Weekly traditions (Shabbat on Friday nights, church on Sunday mornings, etc.)

(Simplicable, 2021)

Which of these traditions are important to you? Much of that list contributed to who I am. My family traditions revolve considerably around food and music. Every event, from celebrations to grief gatherings, involves copious amounts of comfort food and a continuous loop of conversation. I can always count on Mom's banana cake with chocolate frosting for my birthday. That's as much a tradition in my family as *Happy Birthday* in four-part harmony!

Religion and ceremony have established many of our traditions. Can you guess what common denominator exists in nearly all traditional events? Why music, of course! My friend and former colleague Kay Norton (2016) discussed singing and religion/faith in her book, *Singing and Well-Being*. Norton identified "Belief-Based Singing" in various realms of spirituality:

- Singing is prominent in Hinduism, Buddhism (throat singing/chanting), Judaism/Kabbalah/Hasidic, and Christianity.
- Music and dance are primary vehicles for devotion.
- The musical scales and their mathematical proportions reflect Pythagoras' "music of the spheres"—ratios, overtones, and natural phenomena believed to embody God.
- Many faiths believe that singing intensifies and empowers praise/prayer, which helps "tune in" with a deity.
- Singing substantiates the religious experience. In song, beliefs become more tangible.
- There is a physical connection between music and spirituality. Singing resonates many parts of the anatomy—the chest, throat, sinuses, etc.
- Music has the power to change behavior (not only in humans!)
- Singing is an act of praise to God.
- Singing preserves and transmits scripture and holy texts.
- Spiritual singing helps humans endure hardships.

I consider myself to be a spiritual, but not religious person. I am Jewish in my heart, but I don't practice on a regular basis. Mostly, I mooch indescribably scrumdillyumptious Rosh Hashanah and Passover dinners from generous relatives. Again, the food is the tradition, as well as the music. I associate specific foods and songs with specific Jewish holidays, as well as the blessings and sung/chanted prayers. And because I was raised to learn about, respect, and even celebrate holidays and events of other cultures, I imbibe the food and secular music of all of them!

My bat mitzvah was very musical, and my cantor encouraged me to sing most of the service. He also wrote a duet for the occasion, which he performed with Dad. My favorite part of Camp Charles Pearlstein (Jewish overnight camp in the woods of Prescott, AZ) was joining the campfire circle after dinner and singing for hours. Whether I'm dancing the hora to *Hava Nagila* at a wedding or chanting the mourner's kaddish at a funeral, Judaism has played a prominent role in my identity, family, and community.

The same can be said of my choir and musical theater experiences, from elementary school concerts to grownup paid professional gigs. I was learning and writing songs with my bestest, oldest friend, Meri, from the age of ten years on. We had a tradition of sitting at her living room piano for hours, with me on keys, her on guitar, singing folk songs and pop tunes, creating harmonies, and recording our performances (complete with paper-crushing faux applause). Some of those harmonies were established in Meri's backyard pool with marathon floating sessions that resulted in raisin fingertips and kickass vocals. We still have a tradition of making music nearly every time we're together, nowadays during girls' weekends on a porch in the ponderosa pine forest (in our pajamas, with cocktails).

My band's Labor Day weekend camping musical commune extravaganza is a tradition. Sitting on a patio, slurping a cold one, hearing a live blues band while on vacation is a tradition. Singing Christmas carols at the top of our lungs in a sushi bar is a tradition with the hippie chicks (my two BFFs and me). Inviting guests to bang with intention on the gathering drum upon entering my home is a tradition. Blasting loud classic rock on a road trip is a tradition. Soaking in a hot frothy tub with candles and soft classical piano is a tradition.

What are some of your traditions? Why are they meaningful to you? Do they have musical elements? Write them down in a journal. Share them with your loved ones. If you can't think of any, make some of your own. Preserve them. Sing and dance to them. They hopefully summon joyful and sentimental emotions. The next chapter is about how music can evoke a gamut of emotions and why this is important for you, human.

# VII. THERE'S A SONG FOR THAT EMOTION

*"The book of love has music in it. In fact, that's where music comes from. Some of it's just transcendental. Some of it's just really dumb."*
*—Peter Gabriel*

So many different types of emotions influence how we live, interact, and react, the choices we make, the actions we take, and the perceptions we have. Emotions are often characterized by facial expressions (also known as "affect"), body language/physical and physiological responses, verbal reactions/tone of voice, and behaviors. We feel combined emotions. We may experience twenty different emotions before breakfast. These emotions are nuanced and complex. By identifying and understanding the multitude of human emotions, you can gain deeper insight into how emotions are expressed and the impact they have on behaviors.

Psychologists have identified the following basic emotions and their subcategories:

- Joy/Happiness (love, relief, enjoyment, contentment, satisfaction, gratitude, hope, enthusiasm, involvement, curiosity, compassion, confidence, and pride)
- Anger (resentment, rage, jealousy/envy, anxiety, agitation, and stress)
- Sadness (gloom, hopelessness, despair, anguish, depression, distress, and loneliness)
- Shame (guilt, remorse, humiliation, and embarrassment)
- Surprise (amazement, wonder, gratitude, confusion, and unsettlement)
- Fear (fright, terror, anxiety, and worry)
- Disgust (hatred, loathing, contempt, revulsion, rejection, dismissal, and mockery)
- Boredom (complacency and relaxation)

(Verywell, 2021)

Here is an exercise I use with behavioral health patients in discussing emotional management and self-regulation. Take a few minutes and see what comes to mind—or consult your useful playlists.

Different people may interpret music and feel completely different emotions when hearing the same song. Make a list of songs that cause or match the emotions listed below. There is no right or wrong answer. Only your answer. Consider instrumentation and other musical elements, lyrics, associations, and whatever tunes, artists, or genres may come up for you in completing this exercise. Go a step further and try to identify a color with the emotion.

| Emotion | Song, Artist, and/or Genre | Color |
| --- | --- | --- |
| Active | | |
| Alert | | |
| Angry | | |
| Depressed | | |
| Excited | | |
| Festive | | |
| Happy | | |
| Peaceful | | |
| Relaxed | | |
| Romantic | | |
| Scared | | |
| Silly | | |

We all want to experience more joy and love than anger and fear, don't we? I believe music has the power to assist us with that. The more in tune (pun entirely intended) we are with our emotions, the more we connect with music and all forms of art, and connect on a deeper level with other human beings.

**Positive actions to help manage emotions include:**

- Exercising to release endorphins, making you feel better and healthier
- Being kind to others, which helps you to stop worrying about yourself
- Being open and accepting, learning to appreciate what is happening around you, and to avoid excessive criticism of others (and yourself)
- Being mindful—living fully present in the moment
- Talking, spending time with others, and enjoying their company
- Distracting yourself with a good movie, book, or game
- Engaging in the arts…drawing, painting, music, theater, writing, cooking, baking, dancing, etc.
- Not succumbing to negative thinking; if you are experiencing negative thoughts, then challenge them by looking for evidence against them
- Spending time outside, enjoying the fresh air and beauty of nature
- Being grateful
- Playing to your strengths—not only doing things you enjoy, but also doing things that are good for you
- PRESCRIBING MUSIC FOR YOURSELF IN EVERY NOOK AND CRANNY OF YOUR LIFE

In addition to music's connection with emotions, the relationship between music and motivation is telling. I conducted a research project on musical preferences and motivation that I'm going to share with you (abbreviated, you're welcome!), as music can be used to motivate people in several ways and in a variety of situations. Upbeat, energetic music may motivate one to exercise, for example. Slow, sedative music may lull one to relax. Music itself may be used as positive reinforcement, motivating one to complete a task for the reward of listening to or creating music.

## THE ROLE MUSIC PREFERENCES PLAY IN USING MUSIC TO MOTIVATE

While a large body of research supports the connection between music and mood, little definitive evidence of the connection between music and motivation exists. There is also substantial literature on music preferences, but it is evasive in its connection to motivation.

This study was conducted to investigate the relationship between music and motivation, and further, to explore what role music preferences play in that relationship. The research was designed to answer the following questions: Does music motivate people to engage in particular activities or to experience particular emotions? Do people consciously choose to use music to motivate themselves, intentionally selecting specific genres, artists, and/or songs to inspire action or evoke emotion? Do people with a musical background use music as motivation in different ways than those with a non-musical background? Are there variations in music preferences and use of music as motivation among singers—specifically singers of different voice parts? Are there age or gender differences with respect to individual preferences and the use of music as motivation?

Subjects were 129 members of the Arizona State University (ASU) Choral Union. This eclectic group included twenty-five university students, of which eighteen were music majors and seven were non-music majors; nineteen were undergraduate students and six were graduate students. The non-student representation of 104 subjects included three individuals with no musical training, sixteen indicating high school as their highest level of musical training, eighty-four indicating college as their highest level of musical training, and twenty-six unspecified. The overall sample included thirty-eight males and ninety-one females. Ages ranged from eighteen to eighty, with a mean age of forty-nine. Three age groups were considered in the results: twenty-five subjects aged 18-29 ("younger group"), forty-five subjects aged 30-55 ("middle group"), and fifty-nine subjects aged 56+ ("older group"). The choir comprised forty-three sopranos, forty-two altos, eighteen tenors, and twenty-three basses (three subjects did not specify voice part).

The subjects of the choral group sample filled out the questionnaire in the spring of 2003 at a rehearsal setting in a large lecture hall on the ASU campus. Participants were asked to circle all genres of music they listen to, and to rank their top three preferences. The commonly recognized genres, adopted from current *Billboard Magazine* charts and digital television music station listings were alternative, big band/swing, bluegrass, Christian, classic rock, classical, country, dance/club, easy listening, funk, heavy metal, hip-hop, jazz, modern rock, new wave, oldies, opera, pop/Top 40, rap, R&B, show tunes, soul, world music, and "other." The questionnaire also asked if subjects consciously select music for specific occasions, moods, and/or situations. If they answered in the affirmative, they went on to answer whether they listen to specific music for activities such as exercising, doing housework, and relaxing. Respondents had the option of listing genres, artists, and/or songs they listen to when participating in these activities. They were also asked what it is about the music that makes them choose it; for example, lyric content, instrumentation, rhythm, and/or dynamics. Using a five-point ranking scale of "always" to "never," they were asked if they believe music motivates them, if they listen to specific music to improve their mood, and if they listen to specific music to match their existing mood. Finally, they were asked to comment on how they think preferences and attitudes about music determine what people listen to, when, and why. The personal information requested was gender, age, voice part, type of student (music or non-music major/undergraduate or graduate student), and highest level of musical training.

Results indicated no significant differences between music majors and non-music majors, undergraduate and graduate students, or levels of musical training. However, there were some significant findings in comparing gender, age groups, and voice parts.

***Musical genre preference rankings among age groups, based on top three choices:***

| GENRE | YOUNGER (18-29) | MIDDLE (30-55) | OLDER (56+) |
|---|---|---|---|
| Alternative | #1 (tie) | #10 | 0 reported |
| Big Band/Swing | 0 reported | #8 | #5 (tie) |
| Bluegrass | 0 reported | #13 | #13 |
| Christian | #2 | #9 (tie) | #7 |
| Classic Rock | #11 | #3 | #9 |
| Classical | #1 (tie) | #1 | #1 |
| Country | #3 | #9 (tie) | #10 |
| Dance/Club | #8 (tie) | #11 | 0 reported |
| Easy Listening | #6 | #6 (tie) | #5 (tie) |
| Funk | 0 reported | 0 reported | 0 reported |
| Heavy Metal | #13 (tie) | 0 reported | 0 reported |
| Hip-Hop | #10 | #14 | 0 reported |
| Jazz | #7 | #2 | #4 |
| Oldies | #13 (tie) | #9 (tie) | #6 |
| Opera | #9 (tie) | #4 | #2 |
| Pop-Top 40 | #4 | #5 | #12 |
| Rap | 0 reported | 0 reported | 0 reported |
| Rhythm & Blues | #9 (tie) | #9 (tie) | #11 |
| Show Tunes | #8 (tie) | #6 (6) | #3 |
| Soul | 0 reported | #12 (tie) | 0 reported |
| World Music | #9 (tie) | #9 (tie) | 0 reported |
| Other | #12 | #7 | #8 |

The mean response to the question, "Do you believe music motivates you?" was 4.6 on a 5-point scale. Similarly, the mean response to the question, "Do you consciously select specific genres of music for specific occasions, moods, and/or situations?" was 4.2.

The mean response to the question, "Do you listen to specific genres of music to improve your mood?" was 3.7 on the 5-point scale. The mean response to the question, "Do you listen to specific genres of music to match your existing mood?" was also 3.7.

Respondents reported they intentionally listen to music when engaging in some activities. In the overall sample, the most common activities during which music was listened to were driving (93.8%), relaxing (86%), celebrating/feeling happy (79.1%), and cleaning/doing housework (71.3%).

***Percentages of respondents reporting they listen to music while engaging in particular activities:***

| ACTIVITY | YOUNGER (18-29) | MIDDLE (30-55) | OLDER (56+) |
|---|---|---|---|
| Exercise | 72% | 73.3% | 47.5% |
| Cook | 48% | 51.1% | 55.9% |
| Clean/ Do Housework | 92% | 80% | 55.9% |
| Drive | 100% | 97.8% | 88.1% |
| Relax | 76% | 86.7% | 89.8% |
| Work/Study | 48% | 48.9% | 44.1% |
| Celebrate/ Feel Happy | 80% | 91.1% | 69.5% |
| Grieve/Feel Sad | 72% | 66.7% | 61% |

Respondents were asked in an optional column to report any specific genres, artists, and/or songs they intentionally listen to when engaging in the aforementioned activities. Based on respondent suggestions, upbeat, rhythmic, and stimulative music may motivate to get moving and participate in activities including exercising, cleaning/doing housework, cooking, and celebrating. Sedative music may motivate to relax and help with grieving.

Specific genres suggested for exercising included all types of rock, pop/top 40, dance/club, hip-hop, R&B, country, and oldies. Similar suggestions were made for cleaning/doing housework; additional genres included alternative, jazz, big band/swing, Latin, show tunes, and classical. Opera and R&B were commonly listed for cooking; other genres included jazz, country, hip-hop, and classical. All genres were suggested for driving. For relaxing, classical, Christian, jazz, easy listening, and new-age were listed. The genres recommended for working/studying were classical, opera, Christian, jazz, and show tunes. All genres were suggested for celebrating/feeling happy. Genres for grieving/feeling sad were opera, Christian, soft rock, R&B, alternative, country, and show tunes. Finally, sex/romance and eating were written in as "Other" activities in which respondents intentionally listen to music.

The sample used for this study involved musically inclined individuals who have chosen to sing in a large university/community choir. They are likely more interested in and influenced by the classical, opera, and show tunes genres than non-singers, as they regularly study and perform these works. This might explain why classical was ranked the number one preference among all age groups. It was somewhat surprising that hip-hop and rap were not ranked higher among the younger age group, as *Billboard Magazine* has a different story to tell about 18-24-year-olds' preferences. Because these subjects are singers who likely have more sophisticated musical tastes, this group may not be as interested in hip-hop and rap, as compared to their non musically trained peers.

Looking at specific influences on musical preferences, respondents reported that lyric content, instrumentation, rhythm, and dynamics all influence their musical choices, with little variation across the options.

Write-ins for "Other" included melody, harmony, singing voices, language, and specific artists.

The overall results of this study suggest that music almost always motivates people and that individual preferences may play a role in how music motivates people. In summary, this study suggests that most people believe they are motivated by music. People often or always consciously select specific genres of music for specific occasions, moods, and/or situations, although females tend to do this more often than males. Females also listen to specific genres of music to improve their mood, and to match their existing mood more often than males, who do this sometimes.

While some people listen to any music to motivate them, some choose specific music to motivate them to engage in specific activities. Many people intentionally listen to music when driving, relaxing, celebrating/feeling happy, and cleaning/doing housework. The younger and middle age groups are more likely to listen to music while exercising, cleaning/doing housework, and celebrating/feeling happy than the older group. The middle and older age groups are more likely to listen to music when relaxing than the younger group. There is a close division among people who listen to music when working or studying, perhaps because some prefer quiet when trying to concentrate.

Several write-in comments emphasized the belief that music affects mood and has the power to motivate. Another common belief among respondents is that music is linked to memories and emotions. One subject wrote, "Music, like sights and smells, conjures up memories…sometimes we choose specific music to go back to a happy time in our lives." Others wrote that age and family influence music preferences, and that preferences and attitudes about music change with time, maturity, and exposure. Another respondent wrote that familiar music brings comfort, which can be a motivator for listening to specific music. Most people with any musical interest whatsoever would likely agree with a final respondent comment: "I cannot imagine an existence without music!"

The findings in this study can be generalized to the larger population of musically inclined individuals. The sample, however, is not vastly representative of non-musicians, although a minority of individuals in the sample reported little to no musical training. A similar study with a sample group of exclusively non-musical individuals could provide a more accurate cross comparison between musicians and non-musicians.

If music is motivating, we can use it for specific purposes and objectives. That is using music with intention. Here is another exercise I use in the psych environment. Fill it out and keep it on hand so you don't have to think too hard in the moment.

Music can significantly impact your mood and directly affect emotions and behaviors. Try to identify songs you associate with feelings and actions. Does the music change your mood? Does that mood sustain for a while? Do you consciously select music to match your mental state? How can you strategically incorporate music into your life to generate positivity (e.g., using sedative music to relax)?

**Name a song that makes you dance:**

---

(Mine is *Sir Duke*, Stevie Wonder)

**Name a song that makes you cry:**

---

(Mine is *E lucevan le stelle* from *Tosca*, Puccini)

**Name a song that makes you laugh:**

---

(Mine is a tie between *Business Time*, The Flying Conchords and *The Dreidel Song* from South Park's *Mr. Hankey's Christmas Classics*)

**Name a song that motivates you to exercise:**

---

(Mine is anything upbeat…positive *or* angry…rock, pop, Latin, metal)

**Name a song that motivates you to clean/do chores:**

---

(Mine is any stimulative classic/hard/alternative rock, pop)

**Name a song that you like to play in the background when you're working/studying/focusing on the task at hand:**

---

(Mine is silence—no music to distract me physically, intellectually and/or emotionally; one exception: cooking/baking)

**Name a song that makes you anxious/uncomfortable and want to bolt:**

---

(Mine is anything death metal or hardcore gangsta rap)

**Name a song that gets you too much in your head/overthinking/negative thinking:**

---

(Mine is *Numb*, Linkin Park)

**Name a song that triggers sadness, anger, or other unhappy emotions/behaviors:**

---

(Mine is *Tears in Heaven*, Eric Clapton, because it squashes my heart flat every time and as a mother, its content is unthinkable)

**Name a song that helps you find inner strength/feel like a badass:**

---

(Mine is *Free Your Mind*, En Vogue)

**Name a song that you just find really beautiful:**

---

(Mine is *Over the Rainbow/What a Wonderful World*, Israel Kamakawiwo'ole)

**Name a playful song that lifts your spirits:**

---

(Mine is a tie between *Uptown Funk*, Bruno Mars and *Can't Stop the Feeling*, Justin Timberlake)

**What is your guilty pleasure song?**

---

(Mine is *Mmmbop*, Hanson. Please don't tell anyone.)

**What is THE most important song to you? Your go-to song? When all else fails, you play this song and know it will make you feel better.**

---

(Mine is *America* from *West Side Story*, Leonard Bernstein.)

Really, there's a song for just about everything. The following lists reflect my personal favorites, client/patient suggestions, and of course, the internet.

## THERE'S A SONG FOR THAT STRESSOR

- *Bad Ass Jit*, Dee Watkins
- *Banana Pancakes*, Jack Johnson
- *Bigger Picture*, Lil Baby
- *Blue Dream*, Jehne Aike
- *Bring Me to Life*, Evanescence
- *Do Better*, Prezi
- *Don't Worry, Be Happy*, Bobby McFerrin
- *Espionage*, Green Day
- *Feel Good*, Gorillaz
- *Gorilla Biscuits*, Big Mouth
- *Green Light*, NF
- *I Ain't Perfect*, Mozzy
- *Keep Your Head Up*, Andy Grammar
- *Light My Fire*, The Doors
- *Love Vigilante*, New Order
- *Pain Away*, Meek Mill
- *Refuse to Lose*, Cold World
- *Slide*, H.E.R.
- *Suga Suga*, Baby Bash
- *Three Little Birds*, Bob Marley
- *Watch Me Rise*, Have Heart
- *You're Mine Still*, Yung Bleu w/Drake

I once offered a group to a patient who responded with an enthusiastic "Fuck you!" Yup. There's a song for that (*Fuck You*, CeeLo Green). With the lyrics, "Although there's pain in my chest, I still wish you the best with a fuck you," I suppose this is more of a breakup song. Oooh, lots of good tunes for heartbreak!

## THERE'S A SONG FOR THAT BREAKUP

- *Ain't No Sunshine*, Bill Withers
- *Before He Cheats*, Carrie Underwood
- *Blame it on Your Heart*, Patty Loveless
- *Don't Speak*, No Doubt
- *Drinking My Baby Goodbye*, Charlie Daniels
- *Heartbreak Hotel*, Elvis
- *I Can't Make You Love Me*, Bonnie Raitt
- *Jar of Hearts*, Christina Perri
- *Love Hurts*, Nazareth
- *Love Stinks*, J. Geils Band
- *Love Yourself*, Justin Bieber
- *Self Esteem*, The Offsping
- *Since U Been Gone*, Kelly Clarkson
- *Somebody That I Used to Know*, Gotye
- *Someone Like You*, Adele
- *Stay With Me*, Sam Smith
- *Unbreak My Heart*, Toni Braxton
- *When I Was Your Man*, Bruno Mars
- *You Oughta Know*, Alanis Morissette

Let's be a bit more optimistic and list some amazing love songs:

## THERE'S A SONG FOR THAT RELATIONSHIP

- *Ain't Nobody*, Rufus/Chaka Khan
- *Ain't No Mountain High Enough*, Marvin Gaye/Tammi Terrell
- *All of Me*, John Legend
- *All You Need is Love*, Beatles
- *At Last*, Etta James
- *Baby I Love Your Way*, Peter Frampton
- *Be My Baby*, The Ronettes
- *Brighter Than the Sun*, Colbie Caillat
- *Can't Help Falling in Love*, Elvis
- *Cheek to Cheek*, Ella Fitzgerald
- *Cherish*, Madonna
- *Could I Have This Dance*, Anne Murray
- *Count on Me*, Bruno Mars
- *Cowboy Take Me Away*, Dixie Chicks
- *Crazy Love*, Van Morrison
- *Eight Days a Week*, Beatles
- *Endless Love*, Diana Ross/Lionel Richie
- *Eternal Flame*, The Bangles
- *Feels So Right*, Alabama
- *Friday I'm in Love*, The Cure
- *Hallelujah I Love Her So*, Ray Charles
- *Happy Together*, The Turtles
- *Have I Told You Lately*, Van Morrison
- *Heaven*, Bryan Adams
- *Hey Soul Sister*, Train

- *Hey There Delilah*, Plain White Ts
- *How Sweet it Is*, James Taylor
- *I Only Have Eyes for You*, The Flamingos
- *I Say a Little Prayer*, Aretha Franklin
- *I Swear*, John Michael Montgomery
- *I Will Always Love You*, Dolly Parton
- *I'll Be*, Edwin McCain
- *I'll Be There*, Jackson Five
- *I'll Have to Say I Love You in a Song*, Jim Croce
- *Islands in the Stream*, Kenny Rogers/Dolly Parton
- *It Had to Be You*, Harry Connick Jr.
- *Keep On Loving You*, REO Speedwagon
- *Lean on Me*, Bill Withers
- *Love Me Tender*, Elvis
- *Maybe I'm Amazed*, Paul McCartney
- *My Girl*, The Temptations
- *Nobody Does it Better*, Carly Simon
- *One*, U2
- *Perfect*, Ed Sheeran
- *She's Got a Way*, Billy Joel
- *Signed, Sealed, Delivered, I'm Yours*, Stevie Wonder
- *Stand by Me*, Ben E. King
- *Take My Breath Away*, Berlin
- *That's How Strong My Love Is*, Otis Redding
- *The Book of Love*, The Magnetic Fields
- *The First Time Ever I Saw Your Face*, Roberta Flack
- *The Very Thought of You*, Billie Holiday

- *The Way You Make Me Feel*, Michael Jackson
- *This Magic Moment*, The Drifters
- *Top of the World*, The Carpenters
- *Unchained Melody*, Righteous Bros.
- *Unforgettable*, Nat King Cole
- *Vision of Love*, Mariah Carey
- *What is This Thing Called Love*, Frank Sinatra
- *When a Man Loves a Woman*, Percy Sledge
- *Wind Beneath My Wings*, Bette Midler
- *Wonderful Tonight*, Eric Clapton
- *You're Still the One*, Shania Twain
- *Your Love Keeps Lifting Me Higher and Higher*, Jackie Wilson
- *Your Song*, Elton John

What other categories can you come up with? I challenge you right now to name a song for that positive vibe. Better yet, craft a playlist!

As with anything fun and recreational—and therapeutic—please, please, please consider potential triggers. Is there a song that summons an unpleasant memory or even a trauma for you? That song may be your co-worker's favorite and she might play it one day at her desk, a few feet away from you, causing an unpleasant reaction for you. I'll explain.

A *stimulus* rouses activity or energy in someone or something; for example, a person yelling at you or a sudden loud noise. A *trigger* is a thought that we have about a situation, event, or experience; for example, "That person is going to hurt me" or "That noise scared me." When a stimulus occurs, it then leads to a thought that becomes the trigger for behaviors. A *behavior* is the way in which a person responds to a particular situation or stimulus. Examples include flinching, ducking, putting hands up, jumping, heart beating faster, palms sweating, etc.

In the sample situation with you at work, the song is the stimulus, the thought (which might be something like, "The person who hurt me is back for me") is the trigger, and your response (a racing heart or goosebumps) is the behavior. In most cases, we have absolutely no idea what music could be a stimulus that triggers undesirable behavior in others—sometimes even in ourselves. Just think about it. Demi Lovato's *Sober* could be incredibly comforting for someone undergoing chemical dependency treatment, but could be a horrible trigger for someone else in similar circumstances.

That brings me to the final piece of this chapter. I co-authored an article in 2019 with my former student, colleague, and friend, Annamaria Lauderdale-Oliverio, PhD, which I've whittled down mostly to my contribution—a case study I believe illustrates the connection between music and emotions, motivation, and unfortunately, triggers.

## MUSIC THERAPY AND GUITARS FOR VETS: PROMOTING RECOVERY FOR SURVIVORS OF MILITARY SEXUAL TRAUMA

## CHICKS WITH PICKS: THREE MST SURVIVORS AND A COMMUNITY MUSIC THERAPY GROUP

Military Sexual Trauma (MST) is sexual assault or sexual harassment that occurs at any point during an individual's military service (Skjelsbaek, 2001; Suris & Lind, 2008; Skaine, 2016). As with sexual trauma in civilian populations, MST involves disparities in power between the perpetrator and survivor. Forced or coerced sexual encounters, lack of consent, inappropriate sexual remarks or physical contact, and sexual advances or favors are examples of behavior reported by MST (United States Department of Veteran Affairs, 2015). Fear of stigmatization and retaliation from superiors plagues survivors, keeping reports of MST low. Veterans who disclose MST when screened often do not seek MST-related services as MST itself is not a diagnosis; it is an experience and treatment needs are prioritized according to diagnoses provided by healthcare professionals (Schingle, 2009).

Survivors of MST overwhelmingly report symptoms associated with post-traumatic stress disorder (PTSD) as well as other psychological health issues. Sexual assault survivors in both the military and civilian populations show a higher lifetime rate of PTSD for both men (65%) and women (49.5%). Veterans Affairs medical record data indicate that in addition to PTSD, survivors experience mood disorders and substance abuse disorders. However, MST veterans are also notably afflicted with other mental health conditions such as bipolar disorder, schizophrenia, and eating disorders (Northcut & Keinow, 2014; U.S. Department of Veterans Affairs National Center for PTSD, 2015).

Survivors of MST often report difficulties with interpersonal relationships. In some cases, the abuse triggers trust issues, problems engaging in social activities, and sexual dysfunction. It is also common to experience emotional challenges with guilt, shame, and anger over the trauma. Many survivors also indicate hardships in finding or maintaining work after their military service (Conrad, Young & Armstrong, 2014; Brown & Bruce, 2016).

Physical health problems are also prevalent among survivors. Difficulties such as chronic pain, eating disorders, and persistent gastrointestinal problems burden survivors. They also reveal difficulties with attention, concentration, and memory (Suris & Lind, 2008; Turcheck & Wilson, 2010).

Clinicians and researchers have been recognizing the benefits of arts therapies that provide less intensive and intrusive verbal processing interventions. In particular, music therapy provides a flexible, accessible, non-stigmatizing healing environment for treating PTSD symptoms as well as a secure, therapeutic option for addressing sexual trauma experiences.

Community Music Therapy (CoMT) is an approach to working musically with people in context—acknowledging the social and cultural factors of their health, illness, relationships, and music (Ansdell, 2004). Common thematic dynamics in CoMT include spontaneity, elements of performance, high energy, joyful intensity, social/cultural/political context, and larger groups of participants (ten-hundreds). Family, friends, caregivers, and staff members, who are all part of a community, can also participate. Community might mean a neighborhood or geographic location. It might mean a group of individuals through religion, work, or special interests.

The military community, and more specifically—the veteran community, is a larger, more encompassing group of people who share a culture and an honor code. Community leads to solidarity, connections, identification, and transformation. Music in this community setting can create a world as well as represent it, reflect and shape experience.

The CoMT model of the Phoenix chapter of Guitars for Vets, in partnership with Arizona State University since 2012, establishes a safe environment for learning and coping. Music therapy is administered through the educational component of the national program, providing opportunities for social engagement and emotional expression. Veterans receive a minimum of ten sessions of guitar instruction and earn a free guitar and accessories upon completion. Both community and student veterans work closely with ASU music therapy students, who provide instruction as part of their pre-internship clinical training. Many Guitars for Vets graduates continue to play guitar, write songs, and perform, and a number have remained active as volunteers.

The instructional model for Guitars for Vets is "PAGE": patience, acceptance, gratitude, and empathy. There is no exam or pressure to perform. The classes are meant to be enjoyable and the participants learn a skill. It is a means to another end—happiness, fulfillment, and confidence. Veterans with physical disabilities can participate with modifications.

## Background and Protocol

The observations in this article were documented at the ASU Guitars for Vets group during the fall semester of 2018. Sessions ran from mid-September through the end of November in the ASU Music Therapy

Clinic Remo Room. Participants sat in a circle, surrounded by drums and other percussion instruments, a keyboard, and various music visuals, including a Guitars for Vets banner. There were eight participants, four male and four female. According to their self-reported data, three of the four females indicated being survivors of military sexual abuse. This study focuses on the effectiveness of music therapy with the Guitars for Vets program, specifically with these three women, namely, Bev, Rita, and Linda, using participant observations and self-reported data. Analyses of the data were conducted by the supervising board-certified music therapist and three undergraduate music therapy clinical students (acknowledgements and thank you to Taylor Page, Peyton Wayne, and Emily Welsh for their contributions).

At the time the Guitars for Vets group met, **Bev** was a single woman in her early forties and an Army veteran. She had some professional singing/performing and songwriting experience, as well as some basic guitar skills from many years prior. Her primary goal for Guitars for Vets was to be able to accompany herself while singing. In the first few sessions, Bev quickly progressed with her guitar skills in both playing and reading chord sheets.

**Rita** was a single woman in her early sixties and an Army veteran from the Jimmy Carter era. She had experimented with guitar in high school and played piano when she was young. Her goal for Guitars for Vets was to play with others. Rita reportedly had a small plate in her left wrist, which caused some pain and difficulty in playing; however, she remained positive and motivated. Rita was very outspoken throughout the semester and frequently initiated conversation. Rita also reported that she does not have any family.

**Linda** was a single woman in her late thirties, also an Army veteran, from the Operation Enduring Freedom/Operation Iraqi Freedom era. She had some guitar lessons when she was younger. Her goals for Guitars for Vets were to become competent on guitar and to play by ear. Linda was initially very soft-spoken and reserved and was observed by a student instructor as "seemingly uncomfortable in her own skin."

**Jess** was a volunteer instructor who had quite a bit of guitar background, including extensive performance. Jess was a veteran of the Marines Corps, single and in her fifties. She was approximately 5'2" and 100 lbs.—a "tiny warrior and a force to be reckoned with," as described by others in the group.

All participants in the group were veterans of various branches of the United States military. The group was multi-cultural and intergenerational. Some members reported PTSD diagnoses, including the three females of interest who were reportedly MST survivors.

Music therapy for recovery from PTSD resembles traditional music therapy, in which patients are encouraged to make music as part of their healing process. Strengths and needs were evaluated in the first three sessions to determine common goals within the therapy context, which historically included improving socialization, coping skills, and music skills, while common interventions included basic guitar instruction, singing, drumming, songwriting, lyric analysis, relaxation, and improvisation.

Participants completed a musical preferences survey on the first day of instruction. The top genres of music identified were classic rock, country/western, funk, and R&B. These preferences and favorite artists/songs were incorporated into the structure of future sessions. Learning to play the guitar was the primary focus within the context of the CoMT model, fostering an environment of comfort, honesty, confidentiality, learning, and pleasure. The overall treatment goals for this group included improving attention to task, improving musical skills, and increasing socialization.

## Outline of Group Sessions

Ten total sessions were conducted over the course of the semester. The first three served as an assessment period, after which specific goals were established and addressed. While the sessions were tightly structured, the student and volunteer instructors were flexible in adapting to meet the current needs of participants. Typically, sessions began with an introduction/ice breaker activity such as sharing a musical accomplishment, how their practice was going, or sharing a high and low of the week. Next, instructors led the group in learning and reviewing guitar chords and progressions, often with 1:1 breakouts with student and volunteer instructors. Once participants were collectively comfortable to move on, the group played songs together. Verbal processing followed with lyric analysis, sharing of personal experiences or anecdotes, and an assessment of their current emotional state. Finally, a relaxation intervention brought sessions to a close.

### First Session

Over the course of a full semester, all ten of the Guitars for Vets music therapy sessions were documented by three undergraduate music therapy students. The student instructors rotated leadership of interventions to observe the group's behaviors and responses and record data.

Everyone introduced themselves in the first session by stating their name, military branch, years of service, deployment(s), and guitar or general music experience. The group completed the required paperwork and chose a guitar to borrow during the semester. Participants initiated and engaged in socially appropriate introductory conversation. Rita was observed to be vocal and congenially opinionated. At one point she briefly shared that she had grown up in an abusive home and that she was raped in the military. She said she has set out to start a new life and is hopeful for her future. Linda appeared reserved and only participated in discussions when prompted. Even then, she only answered with one word or a short phrase. Bev presented with a bright affect and appeared comfortable socializing. Jess participated in the introductory activities and made small talk with everyone in the room. The anatomy of the guitar and tuning were summarized and the E minor chord was demonstrated.

## Second Session

The second session involved review of the guitar's anatomy, learning to tune with the Guitar Tuna app, fingering and alternating between beginning chords, and learning to read a chord chart. Rita frequently voiced concern over her fingers hurting from practicing. Linda came prepared with a folder for her handouts. Bev was actively engaged throughout the session. Participants were encouraged to create a mnemonic device to remember the order of the strings. Jess shared hers as, "**E**ddie **A**te **D**ynamite, **G**ood-**B**ye **E**ddie," which was received with laughter.

**Aaron**, who did not attend the first session, arrived and made his dominating presence known in the hallway, where the rest of the group was chatting before moving into the classroom. Aaron was a middle-aged male, about 6'3" and over 200 pounds. Upon his arrival, he spoke loudly and interrupted during casual conversation, often turning the subject upon himself. The participants did not seem to be put off by this behavior until he began making jokes and comments that were interpreted as sexist and inappropriate. He said, "I love a babe who can play the guitar" and "Women musicians are so sexy, I just want to kiss them." At this point, Linda quietly left session two without explanation.

Aaron was asked to cease and desist the harassing behavior by the Phoenix Guitars for Vets chapter coordinator in a follow-up phone call, but by hanging up with an expletive, Aaron dismissed himself from the group.

## Third Session

In session three, the returning participants commented that Aaron's behavior was inappropriate and both Rita and Bev shared that he had made them feel extremely uncomfortable. The male participants provided supportive comments to Rita and Bev about not tolerating Aaron's behavior and how everyone should be treated with respect, regardless of gender. Rita and Bev both disclosed that they had considered not returning after the "Aaron incident," but decided to face him if he returned and politely request that he refrain from such language. Both women were visibly relieved when told that Aaron would not be returning. Jess echoed the group's encouraging comments and privately spoke with Rita and Bev after the session to offer further support.

Linda, however, did not return for the third session. The supervising music therapist reached out to Linda in both a phone call and an e-mail. Linda responded via e-mail and reported that Aaron had seriously triggered her PTSD and she did not want to return. After a phone call with methodical verbal processing and gentle persuasion, Linda agreed to return the following week and see how she feels. Upon return, Linda continued to quietly participate but not share emotionally in great depth. She was warmly welcomed and supported, particularly by volunteer Jess, who shared some personal experiences about rising above trauma and always looking to the future. (Linda was able to make up the two sessions she missed by joining the Guitars for Vets Level Two group, which followed the regular weekly groups.)

### Fourth and Fifth Sessions

In the following two sessions, participants learned to play standard guitar chords and corresponding songs. With E minor and A minor, participants were able to play *Ain't No Sunshine* by Bill Withers. This prompted a lyric analysis and discussion about how "people need to go through sad things to get to the happy things." Topics included sadness, love, and loss. Once the participants learned the major A, D, and E chords, they could play Tom Petty's *Free Fallin'*. Again, a lyric analysis was facilitated and participants shared thoughts on relationships, gender roles, and behaviors within dating, what makes a person good or bad, how we perceive others around us, and the meaning of the song's title. One of the male participants said the song is about the stereotype of a nice girl falling for a bad boy. Some reminisced about times in their lives when they felt free. Bev shared that she feels free when she's traveling. Rita expressed that she didn't particularly like this song because she's not a Tom Petty fan but would continue to learn it to be a "team player."

Several participants soon became comfortable enough to sing along as they strummed. Bev consistently sang in tune with a confident tessitura, rich timbre, and supported volume. (*Tessitura* is in relation to the total range of a voice or instrument; *timbre* is the tone "color" or quality, determined by the harmonics of the instrument—in this case, Bev's mezzo-soprano voice. *Supported volume* suggests the effective use of trained and practiced breathing techniques.) She was amenable and generally seemed relaxed, participating and remaining engaged throughout the sessions. Rita often expressed her concern for other participants and whether they were keeping up. Linda continued to be very soft-spoken and generally did not initiate conversation. All participants were improving in their musical skills each week and opening up to each other and the instructors, demonstrating support and camaraderie. During the fifth session, Rita commented that it is difficult to practice at home when she's alone and that she enjoys Guitars for Vets for the social aspect. Also during this session, Bev shared that *Free Fallin'* was stirring up emotions for her because she just went through a breakup and she requested a "happy song." Bev and Jess sat together in this session and throughout the rest of the semester. They seemed to form a natural bond and a friendship blossomed.

### Sixth Session

In the sixth session, the G chord was introduced, as well as *This Land is Your Land* by Woody Guthrie. A lyric analysis about protest, discrimination, and current politics prompted Rita to share that she once participated in a parade that emphasized themes of human rights and equality, where she performed *This Land is Your Land* on a float. She also reported toward the end of the session that this group was helping her positively cope with her PTSD issues. For what was essentially the first time, Linda contributed to a discussion by sharing that the song was powerful and had great meaning for her. She did not elaborate but said she enjoyed singing and playing the song after discussing the meaning. Bev did not share anything personal related to the song but nodded at others' contributions. She strummed and sang the song with accuracy and enthusiasm. Jess provided hand-over-hand assistance to various individuals.

## Seventh Session

During the seventh session, Rita reported that she had been feeling some anxiety about coming to sessions, partly because being in the group was triggering her trauma. She said that despite her feelings, she decided to continue attending and offered insight into how individuals need to be more sensitive and aware of people's feelings because of unknown circumstances. After some probing, she said her previous trauma was the reason. This led to a discussion about coping skills and Rita said she endures her feelings until they pass. Suggested strategies from others included meditation and getting out socially. Bev offered, "Making music."

By the seventh session, participants demonstrated considerable improvement in their musical skills by transitioning chords faster, strumming to tempo, and learning new chords and songs with greater ease. Socially, they were sharing more personal experiences and greeting one another by name. Relationships appeared to be building, as evidenced by friendly gestures such as sharing jokes and patting each other on the back. Considering attention to task, participants were requiring fewer prompts to remain focused and curb side conversation. Linda was the exception, as she remained very quiet and often only responded by nodding her head, seemingly hyper-focused on her guitar.

## Eighth and Ninth Sessions

Learning the twelve-bar blues progression comprised a large portion of the eighth and ninth sessions. Participants learned *Hound Dog* by Elvis Presley and discussed the theoretical background of the progression. They then wrote two original verses to the melody of *Hound Dog* with the theme of dealing with PTSD through music therapy. All clients contributed ideas for lyrics and compromised on suggestions, except for Linda. At one point, Bev quietly told one of the music therapy students that she's a songwriter and didn't like the lyrics about PTSD being written. Jess overheard and politely interrupted the group to suggest that certain lyrics sounded too clinical. At this point, Linda shared that using the word "anxiety" in the lyrics gave her more anxiety. Collectively, lyrics were decided upon and Bev appeared less irritated after Jess validated her feelings and restated her ideas to the group. Linda did not sing the original verses but played along on her guitar, presenting with a flat affect. When a music therapy student played along on a tubano (an Arabic, goblet shaped skin-head drum), Rita asked her to play at a lower volume because, "I can't hear myself think or hear the music at all!"

The ninth session involved rehearsal for the graduation "jam" and reflection on the experience. Rita shared that her previous anxiety and past trauma had prevented her from continuing activities. She often quits things when she starts feeling agitated or has flashbacks of trauma. While she still experiences those anxieties, she said she is learning how to cope with them. She also shared that she likes not having to be a good guitar player and that missing a chord or two is alright. She thanked the group for helping her get past the mental block she experiences when her trauma is triggered. Bev expressed her love for music and how this experience came at the perfect time for her because it helped her cope with a previous abusive relationship and trauma she has dealt with throughout her life. She reported that she found joy in Guitars for Vets and feels as though she has found herself again through re-learning the guitar. Linda simply thanked everyone and said she felt like she had learned a lot.

## Tenth Session

The tenth and final session was graduation, which included a presentation of certificates and guitar packages, a jam session of all the songs learned over the semester, including the original lyrics to the *Hound Dog* twelve-bar blues progression, and a post reception where clients socialized and snacked on the potluck items they shared. All participants appeared excited to explore their new guitars and accessories and expressed their gratitude to peers and instructors. Linda was privately commended by Jess and the supervising music therapist for her courage in continuing with the program after PTSD symptoms were triggered, to which she quietly smiled and nodded.

Bev, Rita, and Linda all developed strong beginning guitar skills and considerably increased their socialization by sharing insights and supporting one another on a deeper level from week to week. All long-term goals were exceeded, particularly those of improved musical skills and increased socialization. Additionally, Bev and Rita demonstrated a wide range of coping skills and emotional regulation, both of which appeared to improve over the semester.

## Discussion

Through the learning of basic guitar skills, live music-making, lyric analysis, and songwriting within a CoMT structure, the Guitars for Vets participants—Bev, Rita, and Linda, in particular—all achieved the long-term goals of the semester to improve attention to task, improve musical skills, and increase socialization. By the end of ten sessions, the group was better able to control interruptions and follow through with assigned tasks. Each participant successfully learned to play and alternate between seven common chords and perform five full songs. Socialization improved every week with all participants establishing a strong rapport and substantively opening up more and more as the semester progressed. Discussion topics included coping mechanisms, anger management, self-awareness, change, practice methods, support systems, relationships, patriotism, and the future. Music chosen to learn and perform reflected participants' reported preferences, which likely encouraged higher participation and engagement. The learning of new chords and varying interventions made for challenging work that led to a strong sense of accomplishment, increased self-esteem, and unity. Despite some humorous self-deprecation, participants reportedly felt like better musicians at the end of the program. Many commented on how much they enjoyed the camaraderie and spirit of the group. All three of the women focused upon in this study made significant personal and musical strides. **Rita** consistently participated and was extremely vocal throughout the semester. She shared very private personal experiences about both her family history and her MST. She reportedly made progress in dealing with her PTSD and chose to face it rather than hide from it. **Bev** demonstrated consistent progress in her guitar skills but really came alive with singing opportunities. Bev and Jess have maintained a friendship and started playing music together as a duo. They are now searching for a drummer and bass player to form a female veteran band for songwriting, performing, and fundraising. Returning to the group after the "Aaron incident" was a significant breakthrough for **Linda** and possibly the defining music therapy moment of the overall experience.

Despite the threatened setback in session two, Aaron's departure promoted a sense of solidarity among the remaining participants as they discussed his problematic behavior. The three MST survivors felt validated and supported by the group. It is within this environment of support that the three female survivors were able to accomplish their learning goals and two of them were able to verbally process through their reactions.

## Conclusion

Music therapy is a useful therapeutic tool to reduce symptoms of PTSD and improve functioning among individuals who have been exposed to sexual trauma. Through diverse song interventions such as lyric analysis and composition, verbal processing can take place on difficult topics such as love, anxiety, sadness, patriotism, politics, and loss. In addition, music therapy can provide an appropriately flexible and supportive environment, engaging individuals who might otherwise struggle with the stigma often associated with mental health and seeking professional help. While further rigorous empirical study is needed, this pilot research suggests the value of integrating music therapy into clinical practice when treating survivors of MST because of its effectiveness in addressing trauma symptoms within a safe and healing social environment.

Music associations are not only related to emotions, but also to memory. We will explore the relationship and connection between music and memory in the next chapter.

# VIII. THERE'S A SONG FOR THAT MEMORY

*"It's something unpredictable, but in the end it's right. I hope you had the time of your life." —Green Day*

My choir performed Whitney Houston's *Greatest Love of All* at my high school graduation, so I make that association every time I hear the song. During the holidays, *O Holy Night* makes me think of my dad because I have never heard anyone perform it more beautifully than he did. Anything Boston reminds me of ditching high school junior year to tube down the Salt River. George Michael's *Faith* album brings me back to shameless merrymaking in Peterson Hall at Northern Arizona University. Van Halen, the Eagles, Billy Joel, and Manhattan Transfer are always reminiscent of road trips. These are only a few of my personal connections between music and the brain's memory centers.

I have witnessed individuals with Alzheimer's and dementia, who haven't spoken a word in months, completely light up with music and sing every word to a familiar song. They oftentimes experience a brief reprieve from their symptomology with moments of clarity, nostalgia, and recollection. Imagine how precious these fleeting moments are for loved ones to witness.

Music and memory are intricately linked. Music is a pleasurable, emotional event that facilitates memory formation and retrieval. The memory of a present emotional state becomes a feeling, which is then associated with music. My pal Barb Crowe (2004) said, "Having a feeling response to a particular piece of music comes from a process of conditioned response. The music is linked to certain memories, and we become conditioned to have that certain feeling when we hear the music again."

The functions of memory are carried out in the brain by the hippocampus and other related structures in the temporal lobe. The hippocampus and amygdala form part of the limbic system, which supports a variety of functions such as emotion, behavior, and long-term memory. It is a pathway in the brain for the signals that underlie emotions. The hippocampus is a complex brain structure with a major role in learning, emotional memory, spatial memory, recall, and regulation. It codes and encodes memory, relating short-term memory to long-term memory. The amygdala generates emotion, which is an important part of memory formation. This is where emotions are given meaning and remembered. It also plays a primary role in decision-making and emotional responses. Fun fact: brain wave states similar to REM sleep are generated during deep music listening experiences and may function to solidify memory (Crowe, 2004). Music influences and acts as a context for memory.

Neurologist and music enthusiast Oliver Sacks (2007) discussed the reliability of musical memory. "The imagining of music, even in relatively nonmusical people, tends to be remarkably faithful not only to the tune and feeling of the original, but to its pitch and tempo. Underlying this is the extraordinary tenacity of musical memory, so much of what is heard during one's early years may be engraved on the brain for the rest of one's life. Our auditory systems, our nervous systems, are indeed exquisitely tuned for music."

## TYPES OF MEMORY

- *Short-term memory* only lasts 20-30 seconds. It stores information temporarily and then either dismisses it or transfers it to long-term memory. Short-term memory is different from working memory, which is more specific to information we receive, use quickly, then discard, for example, a name, phone number, short grocery list, something in the open refrigerator that will not return to your mind no matter how long you stare at it, the song someone just asked you to play but you forget by the time you tap Spotify, etc.
- *Long-term memory* is anything that happened more than a few minutes ago. Two types: explicit and implicit.
- *Explicit* memories are thought about consciously (e.g., the name of your childhood dog or your best friend's address). Two types: episodic and semantic.
- *Episodic memory* relates to our personal lives (e.g., your grandparents surprising you on Christmas morning, your wedding day, your championship game, etc.). Episodic memories are not always accurate because we tend to reconstruct them over time. Our ability to retain episodic memories depends on how emotionally powerful the experiences were (e.g., What were you doing when you heard JFK was shot? Where were you when you saw video of the first plane strike the World Trade Center's north tower on 9/11?).
- *Semantic memory* accounts for our general knowledge of the world (e.g., the sky is blue, an elephant has a trunk, we must pay taxes, etc.). Semantic memory is more reliable than episodic memory because we can maintain the accuracy and strength of our semantic memory over time, although it begins to slowly decline with age.

- *Implicit memory* involves memories you do not have to consciously recall (e.g., riding a bike, speaking a language, etc.). With a lot of conscious thought while learning, it becomes implicit automatically.
- *Procedural memory* is a type of implicit memory, which allows us to perform certain tasks without thinking about them (e.g., tying your shoe, brushing your hair, driving your car, etc.).

To sharpen your memory, take tests, play brain games, get plenty of sleep, engage all your senses, minimize caffeine, minimize stress, minimize distractions, maintain a healthy diet, drink tons of water, and exercise (Predictive Safety, 2021). Don't forget music as a sensory input!

Let's talk music and entertainment. *Animal House* isn't *Animal House* without *Louie Louie* by The Kingsman, right? Quick! Match the hit song with its companion film:

- *Can You Feel the Love Tonight?*
- *Can't Stop the Feeling*
- *City of Stars*
- *Don't You Forget About Me*
- *I Don't Want to Miss a Thing*
- *I Will Always Love You*
- *Lose Yourself*
- *Mrs. Robinson*
- *My Heart Will Go On*
- *Old Time Rock & Roll*
- *Take My Breath Away*
- *The Power of Love*
- *Unchained Melody*

- *Up Where We Belong*
- *Wind Beneath My Wings*
- *You've Got a Friend in Me*

These songs became synonymous with the movies they were featured in. Many of our favorite songs are associated with our favorite movies. Anytime I hear a song from a great movie, I have an instant memory of the scene it was in, such as *Pretty Woman* Julia Roberts grooving in the bathtub to Prince's *Kiss*. I might even remember something peripheral and seemingly insignificant—what theater I saw the movie at, with whom, what I was wearing, what we ate—stored away in that complex brain of mine.

Some of my favorite soundtracks:

- *10 Things I Hate About You*
- *A Clockwork Orange*
- *Almost Famous*
- *American Graffiti*
- *The Big Chill*
- *Boogie Nights*
- *Dirty Dancing*
- *The Electric Horseman*
- *Forrest Gump*
- *Good Fellas*
- *Guardians of the Galaxy Awesome Mix Vol. 1*
- *Jersey Boys*
- *Kill Bill Vol. 1 & 2*
- *Brother, Where Art Thou?*
- *Pulp Fiction*
- *Purple Rain*

- *Saturday Night Fever*
- *Singles*
- *Sleepless in Seattle*
- *When Harry Met Sally*

Now match the TV theme song lyrics with the show:

- *"Boy, the way Glenn Miller played songs that made the hit parade..."*
- *"Come and knock on our door, we've been waiting for you..."*
- *"Here's the story of a lovely lady, who was bringing up three very lovely girls..."*
- *"Just sit right back and you'll hear a tale, a tale of a fateful trip..."*
- *"Love, exciting and new, come aboard, we're expecting you..."*
- *"Making your way in the world today takes everything you've got..."*
- *"Oh baby, I hear the blues a-callin', tossed salad and scrambled eggs..."*
- *"So no one told you life was gonna be this way..."*
- *"The animals, the animals, trap, trap, trap 'til the cage is full..."*

How about *Andy Griffith*'s whistle and the instrumentals you immediately associate with the show? *The Addams Family, ER, Hawaii Five-O, Hill Street Blues, I Dream of Jeannie, Looney Tunes, M*A*S*H*, Sex and the City, The Simpsons, The X-Files,* and countless others.

I always remember a great live show. Again, insignificant or not, all it takes it a song and I can recall the venue, who I was with, what I was wearing, what cognition-altering elements may have been involved, any shenanigans that ensued, and how bad the tinnitus was next morning. I'll never forget seeing *Phantom of the Opera* for the first time in Los Angeles—with Michael Crawford. Tears were dripping from my binoculars! In

1997 London, I saw three performances in one day—*Damn Yankees*, *Les Misérables* (where every performer who stepped on stage was even better than the last), and *Miss Saigon*. Oh, *Miss Saigon*. I was alone, sitting next to a woman who was with her husband or significant other. Throughout the performance, he had his arms crossed with a stoic look on his face. The woman quietly reacted during various scenes and I got the sense that she was squashing her emotion for his sake. If you know the musical and you know how it ends, you also know that it is not humanly possible to NOT have an emotional response. Apart from that man. When the big moment happened, the woman next to me and I grabbed each other's hands and squeezed for a good couple minutes before we let go, looked at each other with tears in our eyes, strangers, and smiled. That was our entire interaction, but boy was it powerful!

I have some amazing concert memories. The floor was shaking with Stevie Wonder—the very best concert I ever attended! I got nailed on the forearm with a full water bottle at Faith No More/Guns N' Roses/Metallica, which left an impressive bruise. I partied with AC/DC when I was eighteen and cute. My friends and I were gifted backstage passes to meet the band. They were short. At a different venue, outdoors in the blazing flames of Phoenix summer, I walked around decked out in a leather miniskirt, heels, and tall '80s hair (what a moron) at Pink Floyd. I completely lost myself in the improvisational vibe at a Dave Matthews Band concert. I chipped a tooth on pretzel salt with U2. I sang every single word to every single song along with the rest of the geriatric audience at the last Eagles concerts I attended (six months before Glenn Frey died). I met the glorious Keith Lockhart of the Boston Pops after he conducted a performance at Phoenix Symphony Hall. I bawled my eyes out when Jason Mraz performed *I Won't Give Up* because I was in the process of filing for divorce and had definitely given up. At an intimate Primus concert, everyone bounced like pogo sticks for the entire show. Another favorite concert memory is when I was pouring my smuggled-in beer into my obligatory red solo cup at a Bob Seger concert back in the late '80s. I got busted by the security guard, who took the can, looked left and right, poured the rest of it in my cup, crushed the can, winked at me, and walked away. I feared for Charlie Daniels' heart when he performed all bloated and sweaty outdoors in over 100-degree heat. This was part of Country Thunder in the mid '90s when the newspaper I worked for sponsored the event. I was part of the exclusive VIP club (aren't you impressed?) and met the likes of Tim McGraw, LeAnn Rimes, John Michael Montgomery, Tanya Tucker, and Reba McEntire. My team and I lived in an RV for three days at this event and engaged in all kinds of colorful debauchery. I wrote a song about it afterwards that goes a little somethin' like this:

**AIN'T NOBODY'S BUSINESS**

The scene was set for lovin' on the night we met.

All the liquor flowin' went straight to my head.

You rapidly became the finest prospect in the room.

Had I known the consequence would be my reputation,

I never would've reeled you in with my flirtation.

Now you opened up your mouth and yapped about way too soon.

It ain't nobody's business. Ain't nobody's business.

Ain't nobody's business. Ain't nobody's business.

Because what happened happened, it was only you and me.

So zip your lip, then lock it tight and throw away the key.

Remember how we shut the door so no one else could see?

It ain't nobody's business except for you and me.

Blab, blab, blab, blab, blab, blab, blab, blab,

Ain't nobody's business except for you and me.

Well, now I'm the target of everybody's questions,

And this ain't the first time, I never learn my lesson,

But humiliation like this, I never suffered before.

Looking back now, your performance wasn't worth it.

Don't bother me again, made up my mind, I gotta split.

So shut your yap for good, 'cus you ain't braggin' no more.

It ain't nobody's business. Ain't nobody's business.

Ain't nobody's business. Ain't nobody's business.

Because what happened happened, it was only you and me.

So zip your lip, then lock it tight and throw away the key.

Remember how we shut the door so no one else could see?

It ain't nobody's business except for you and me.

Blab, blab, blab, blab, blab, blab, blab, blab,

Ain't nobody's business except for you and me.

You can probably ascertain the song's inspiration. Let's just move on. Memories and associations are mental connections, but they are not synonymous. Memory is the faculty by which the mind stores and recalls information. Association is a relationship between two ideas, events, feelings, etc., where one activates a representation of another...a memory. Association is at the root of all learning. Human thought would not be possible without things already known and present in our memory, compared with new experiences. We assign meaning through associations as a mental scheme with sequencing and networking.

Our associations are often music-based. The first dance song at my wedding was Al Greene's *Let's Stay Together*. We didn't. But both the memory and the association are always there and activated anytime I hear the song. Following are lists of songs that have been associated with various categories, generated for themed music therapy groups I have facilitated in the behavioral health hospital:

## SONGS ASSOCIATED WITH MINDFULNESS AND POSITIVITY

- *Adventure of a Lifetime*, Coldplay
- *Best Day of My Life*, American Authors
- *Can't Stop the Feeling*, Justin Timberlake
- *Count on Me*, Bruno Mars
- *Don't Worry, Be Happy*, Bobby McFerrin
- *Dynamite*, BTS
- *Five Thousand Miles*, The Proclaimers
- *Geronimo*, Sheppard
- *Good Days*, SZA
- *Good Time*, Owl City/Carly Rae Jepsen
- *Happy*, Pharrell
- *Haven't Met You Yet*, Michael Bublé
- *Hey Soul Sister*, Train
- *Hey Ya!*, Outkast
- *High Hopes*, Panic at the Disco
- *I Gotta Feeling*, Black Eyed Peas
- *Imagine*, John Lennon
- *Just Dance*, Lady Gaga/Colby O'Donis
- *Keep Your Head Up*, Andy Grammer
- *Lean on Me*, Bill Withers
- *Let it Be*, The Beatles
- *Love Song*, Sara Bareilles
- *On Top of the World*, Imagine Dragons
- *Over the Rainbow/What a Wonderful World*, Israel Kamakawiwo'ole

- *Party in the USA*, Miley Cyrus
- *Put Your Records On*, Corrine Bailey Rae
- *She Looks So Perfect*, 5 Seconds of Summer
- *Shut Up and Dance*, Walk the Moon
- *Skyscraper*, Demi Lovato
- *Smile*, Lily Allen
- *Sunday Morning*, Maroon 5
- *Sunflower*, Post Malone
- *There's Nothing Holding Me Back*, Shawn Mendes
- *Three Little Birds*, Bob Marley
- *Thunder*, Imagine Dragons
- *Time of Your Life*, Greenday
- *Uptown Funk*, Bruno Mars
- *Wannabe*, Spice Girls

## SONGS ASSOCIATED WITH SELF-ACCEPTANCE AND SELF-LOVE

- *All About that Bass*, Meghan Trainor
- *Beautiful*, Christina Aguilera
- *Bitch*, Meredith Brooks
- *Born This Way*, Lady Gaga
- *Brave*, Sara Bareilles
- *Bulletproof*, La Roux
- *Feeling Myself*, Nicki Minaj
- *Fight Song*, Rachel Platten
- *Good as Hell*, Lizzo
- *Hands*, Jewel

- *Hold On*, Alabama Shakes
- *Hollaback Girl*, Gwen Stefani
- *I Am Woman*, Helen Reddy
- *I Will Survive*, Gloria Gaynor
- *Imperfection*, Saving Jane
- *Irreplaceable*, Beyoncé
- *Never Said*, Liz Phair
- *Perfect*, Pink
- *Play God*, Ani DeFranco
- *Praying*, Kesha
- *Respect*, Aretha Franklin
- *Roar*, Katy Perry
- *Royals*, Lorde
- *Scars to Your Beautiful*, Alessia Cara
- *Shake it Off*, Taylor Swift
- *Stranger*, KC
- *Superwoman*, Alicia Keys
- *This is Me*, Keala Settle
- *Titanium*, David Guetta
- *Try*, Colbie Caillat
- *Unpretty*, TLC
- *Video*, India Arie
- *You Should See Me in a Crown*, Billie Eilish

(Any coincidence that most of these artists are female? I think not!)

## SONGS ASSOCIATED WITH BEHAVIORS, HOPE, AND CHANGE

- *A Change is Gonna Come*, Sam Cooke
- *All Things Past*, George Harrison
- *Believer*, Imagine Dragons
- *Breakaway*, Kelly Clarkson
- *Breathe Me*, Sia
- *Carry On*, Crosby/Stills/Nash & Young
- *Change the World*, Eric Clapton
- *Change*, Blind Melon
- *Changes*, Chubby Checker
- *Changes*, David Bowie
- *Demons*, Imagine Dragons
- *Don't Dream it's Over*, Crowded House
- *Don't Stop Believin'*, Journey
- *Don't You Worry Child*, Swedish House Mafia
- *Drive*, Incubus
- *Dust in the Wind*, Kansas
- *Everybody Hurts*, R.E.M.
- *Eye of the Tiger*, Survivor
- *Fake Happy*, Paramore
- *Fighting My Way Back*, Thin Lizzy
- *Fire and Rain*, James Taylor
- *Hallelujah*, Leonard Cohen
- *I Can*, Nas
- *I Want to Break Free*, Queen
- *I'll Take You There*, The Staple Singers

- *I'm Still Standing*, Elton John
- *If Everyone Cared*, Nickelback
- *Man in the Mirror*, Michael Jackson
- *Move on Up*, Curtis Mayfield
- *Movin' On*, Rascal Flatts
- *One Love*, Bob Marley
- *Reach Out I'll be There*, The Four Tops
- *Revolution*, The Beatles
- *Smile*, Nat King Cole
- *Swim*, Jack's Mannequin
- *The Times They Are-a-Changin'*, Bob Dylan
- *Turn! Turn! Turn!*, The Byrds
- *We Shall Overcome*, Joan Baez
- *Wild World*, Cat Stevens
- *Wind of Change*, The Scorpions
- *With My Own Two Hands*, Ben Harper
- *Won't Back Down*, Tom Petty
- *You Gotta Be*, Des'ree

## SONGS ASSOCIATED WITH DEPRESSION

- *Away from the Sun*, 3 Doors Down
- *Basket Case*, Green Day
- *Be OK*, Ingrid Michaelson
- *Behind Blue Eyes*, The Who
- *Breathe Me*, Sia
- *Car Radio*, twenty one pilots
- *Comfortably Numb*, Pink Floyd

- *Creep*, Radiohead
- *Dark Times*, The Weeknd
- *Day 'N Nite*, Kid Cudi
- *Down in a Hole*, Alice in Chains
- *Every Night*, Paul McCartney
- *Everybody Hates Me*, The Chainsmokers
- *Fade to Black*, Metallica
- *Fell on Black Days*, Soundgarden
- *Gravity*, John Mayer
- *Have You Ever Seen the Rain*, CCR
- *Here Comes the Rain Again*, Eurythmics
- *Here Comes the Sun*, The Beatles
- *Hurt*, Nine Inch Nails
- *I Can See Clearly Now*, Johnny Nash
- *I'm Only Happy When It Rains*, Garbage
- *It's Been Awhile*, Staind
- *Lithium*, Evanescence
- *Lovely*, Billie Eilish/Khalid
- *Mercy Street*, Peter Gabriel
- *No Rain*, Blind Melon
- *Nobody Knows*, Pink
- *Paint it Black*, Rolling Stones
- *Redemption Song*, Bob Marley
- *Runaway Train*, Soul Asylum
- *Runaway*, Kanye West
- *Summertime Sadness*, Lana Del Rey
- *The Dark Side*, Muse

- *Turn Blue*, The Black Keys
- *Unwell*, Matchbox 20
- *Zero*, Imagine Dragons

## SONGS ASSOCIATED WITH ADDICTION AND RECOVERY

- *After I've Lost it All*, Max Flinn
- *Amazing*, Aerosmith
- *Angel*, Sarah McLaughlin
- *Bad*, U2
- *Breaking the Habit*, Linkin Park
- *Cocaine*, Jackson Browne
- *Cold Turkey*, John Lennon
- *Dark Times*, The Weeknd
- *Demons*, Kenny Chesney
- *Detox Mansion*, Warren Zevon
- *Going Through Changes*, Eminem
- *Gravity*, A Perfect Circle
- *Hate Me*, Blue October
- *How Could You Leave Us*, NF
- *I Surrender*, Hillsong
- *It Ain't Me*, Kygo
- *Kiss from a Rose*, Seal
- *Master of Puppets*, Metallica
- *Mr. Brownstone*, Guns N' Roses
- *Not an Addict*, K's Choice
- *One Day at a Time*, Joe Walsh
- *Otherside*, Macklemore

- *Recovery*, James Arthur
- *Rehab*, Amy Winehouse
- *Rehab*, Machine Gun Kelly
- *Relapsing*, Beartooth
- *Running to Stand Still*, U2
- *Sober*, Demi Lovato
- *Sober*, Pink
- *Sober*, Tool
- *Starting Over*, Macklemore/Ryan Lewis
- *The A Team*, Ed Sheeran
- *The Hunger*, Florence and the Machine
- *The More I Drink*, Blake Shelton
- *Under the Bridge*, Red Hot Chili Peppers
- *You Don't Know Jack*, Luke Bryan
- *You Found Me*, The Fray

You likely have many songs to add to these lists. Do it! Create your own playlists for whatever you're feeling, experiencing, or imagining. You can also make playlists to change your mood. If you wake up in the morning feeling down, validate it. Honor it. Make a playlist of depressing songs. Then turn it around and make a playlist for positivity.

Music's connection to emotion, memory, and associations may result in songs bringing certain people to mind. I love the stories about music and people coming up in the next chapter.

# IX. THERE'S A SONG FOR THAT PERSON

*"Come on people now, smile on your brother. Everybody get together and try to love one another right now." —The Youngbloods*

Do you hear a song and immediately think of someone? Whenever I hear Toto's *Africa*, I think of my friend and former colleague Kristina. We were in my little red Toyota pickup truck, returning to work at the newspaper from lunch and, of course, had to wait for the song to end before getting out. We cranked the volume, sang from our guts, drummed the dashboard, and shared that moment of human musical joy. I have numerous jams that are exclusive to specific people.

My friend Cara and I listened to Lenny Kravitz's *5* album for the first time while driving in the 'hood of south-central Phoenix to Los Dos Molinos for dinner. We flew down Baseline Rd. to *Fly Away* and had headbanger's neck the next morning.

Tim, my first real love, and I were the ultimate-envy-of-all-spectators karaoke couple. Sonny & Cher's *I've Got You Babe* was our signature tune and I always think of him when I hear it.

Carolyn and I became BFFs the first day of high school. She is synonymous with every song (and scene) from *Purple Rain* and *Footloose* to *Candide* and *Phantom of the Opera.*

When my daughter was a very small person, I heard her coughing in her room and investigated. Just as I entered, she projectile vomited while *Let it Go* from *Frozen* was playing on her sticker-clad pink boom box. She let it go indeed and years later, I think of it every time I hear or sing the song (I sing it several times a week with clients, unfortunately).

Franklin, a patient at the psych hospital, insisted on going to the gym, even though his clothes were in the dryer. He came in a hospital gown. Inevitably, while playing volleyball, Franklin ended up on his back with his legs in the air. We all just laughed and made light of it. What else can you do? We had the bonus of Miley Cyrus' *Party in the USA* in the background, which we changed to "Mishap in the gym that day."

I visited Norman in a palliative care unit shortly before his death. He was sharing a curtain-separated room with a man who continued to increase the volume on the TV to drown out our interaction. I politely and repeatedly asked the roommate to lower the volume, but he refused and started tossing insults ("I didn't ask to listen to this crap!"). A nurse entered and rolled Grumpelstiltskin right out of the room and down the hall, where we could still hear his protests, but they were no longer disruptive. I played guitar and sang gentle old cowboy and folk tunes, which Norman had non-verbally indicated as preferences. A few tears rolled down his weathered face and he smiled at me with his cloudy blue eyes. Just as we were wrapping things up, the roommate returned and muttered something colorful. Once Grumpy was re-situated, Norman slowly reached out, pulled back the curtain, and vigorously extended his middle finger. Good times. And a consistent visual for *Red River Valley.*

Also as a hospice music therapist, I visited Walt, who was actively dying. I sang at his bedside with his wife, Judy, standing on the other side of the bed. Walt had that rattled breathing often heard when one is close to the end. His eyes were closed, his face sunken. Judy requested song after song—those she knew to be Walt's favorites. She sang to him, held his hand, and bent down to whisper in his ear. She said things like, "Let go if you're ready," "I'm going to be okay," "We did pretty good, didn't we?" While singing *Bye Bye Blackbird*, Walt raised his eyebrows. Judy bent down and put her ear to his lips, but he said nothing. He arched his neck, touched his forehead to Judy's, then took his final breath and was gone. I wasn't kidding when I said this is meaningful work. Judy later tracked me down and thanked me with hugs and tears. She told me she believed that through the music experience, Walt found permission to surrender. She said it was a beautiful ending and she wouldn't have wanted it any other way.

I have a few hospice stories to share with you that represent songs I associate with people: two formally written pieces and a couple unadorned anecdotes. Hospice is beautiful work. I am often asked if it's depressing, but I find it an honor to improve someone's quality of life in their final days, weeks, or months, not to mention the bereavement work with loved ones.

I believe every client/patient I interact with should be celebrated, regardless of background, race, ethnicity, religion, sexuality, political affiliation, shape, size, and bank account. I am an ally and an advocate. I believe you should be who you are, love who you love, and live how you want (within law and reason!). Let your freak flag fly and if someone doesn't like it, they can piss right straight off!

So many personalities. So many narratives. I have crossed paths with countless people in my music therapy work and every one of them has a story...and a song.

## INFORMAL VIGNETTE: SONGWRITING WITH A TERMINALLY ILL GENTLEMAN AND HIS WIFE

Sam was a terminally ill patient receiving services through Sunrise Health and Hospice. He and his wife requested music therapy and Sam's nurse made the referral in early 2012. Sam continued to qualify for hospice services with Sunrise, so a strong rapport was established between Sam, his wife, and the therapist. This vignette is taken from two consecutive sessions in July of 2012.

## Clinical Setting

A residential group home in Apache Junction, AZ. Weekly sessions were conducted at bedside in the patient's room, which was small and clean with abundant natural light.

## Client(s)

Sam was a ninety-three-year-old Caucasian male with a diagnosis of "unspecified debility." Sam's wife, Caroline, was almost always present at the weekly music therapy sessions. Sam and Caroline were Roman Catholic and attended church on a regular basis before Sam was placed in hospice care. They traveled the world together and were active supporters of the arts, frequently attending classical music and opera performances.

Sam and Caroline were a living example of a true love story. They were both widowed and eventually made their way to Arizona—Sam from New York and Caroline from Minnesota. They met through a mutual friend who sent Sam to Caroline's house to help her set up her VCR (he is a retired electrical engineer). They took an immediate and unexpected liking to each other and as they say, "The rest is history!"

Ongoing goals for Sam included providing comfort, enhancing quality of life, elevating spirits, promoting relaxation, expressing emotions, and engaging in life review/reminiscence. The following intervention targeted expression of emotions, life review/reminiscence, and improved quality of life.

## The Sessions/Intervention

Sam and Caroline held nothing back about their feelings for each other. They had numerous terms of endearment for one another and "I love you" was expressed both verbally and non-verbally (with tender looks, handholding, etc.) throughout sessions. They both were generous in sharing their history and their love story with the therapist, often through tears, and music therapy sessions were typically structured around singing of love songs, hymns, and favorite oldies/standards, which served as a catalyst for discussion and reminiscence.

In the first of these two sessions, the therapist suggested that Sam and Caroline write a love song to each other. While Caroline sang and played piano, she said she didn't know how to write music and appeared somewhat reluctant. The therapist assured her that her and Sam's words were the most important component to this exercise and several love songs were then sung together to emphasize that idea. Sam, Caroline, and the therapist sang *Let the Rest of the World Go By*, *Love Me Tender*, *Can't Help Falling in Love with You*, *I Love You Truly*, *Always*, *Let Me Call You Sweetheart*, *Down by the Old Mill Stream*, *The Sweetest Story Ever Told*, and *My Blue Heaven*. After singing all these songs together (with many tears from Caroline) and briefly analyzing lyrics, Sam requested his favorite song for Caroline, *The 12th of Never* (in the style of Johnny Mathis). He enthusiastically sang the entire song and said he wished he had written it. It was then decided that the song they would write for each other would be to the tune of *The 12th of Never* to establish a sense of security through familiarity.

The therapist facilitated a discussion that highlighted how Sam and Caroline met, what they love about each other, and how their relationship is unique from others. Using Sam's and Caroline's verbal contributions, the therapist generated lyrics and added several verses to the original song. The original lyrics are as follows:

**THE 12TH OF NEVER**

You ask how much I need you, must I explain?

I need you, oh, my darling, like roses need rain.

You ask how long I'll love you, I'll tell you true.

Until the twelfth of never, I'll still be loving you.

**CHORUS:**

**Hold me close. Never let me go. Hold me close. Melt my heart like April snow.**

I'll love you 'til the bluebells forget to bloom.

I'll love you 'til the clover has lost its perfume.

I'll love you 'til the poets run out of rhyme.

Until the twelfth of never, and that's a long, long time.

CHORUS

Following are the additional verses written together by Sam, Caroline, and the therapist, keeping the original chorus in between verses:

(Sam's verses to Caroline)

She's nice to everybody, so much in love with me.

We traveled everywhere together and enjoyed the symphony.

She's the kindest, sweetest lady I ever knew.

She's my definition of love, and lovely to look at too!

CHORUS

A wonderful musician, taught piano and sang in the church choir.

She's been awfully good to me and sets my heart afire.

Caroline, I love you, I know that you can see

That you're the very best thing that ever happened to me.

CHORUS

(Caroline's verses to Sam)

My first Christmas in Arizona, that's when we first met.
You set up my VCR, who knew we'd be so fortunate?
Married later in life, we hoped for five years.
Now we're at twenty-five, so many happy tears.

CHORUS

We have so much in common, church and music we always share.
It's almost too good to be true, all this love and tender care.
Our partnership is different, it's love without words or rules.
Oh Sam, I thank you for your love, I've known nothing more true.

CHORUS

After the song was crafted, the therapist sang it for Sam and Caroline, accompanied with guitar. They actively listened, held hands, smiled at each other, and cried. When the song ended, they both emphatically thanked the therapist and asked for a copy of the lyrics. The therapist promised that along with an extra surprise at the next session.

When the therapist returned the following week, she presented Sam and Caroline with copies of the lyrics and a recording of the song (the therapist included on the CD a few hymns that Sam frequently requested). They sang their song together and discussed the process of songwriting and what it accomplished for them as a couple, especially in this difficult time of uncertainty and impending loss. It was an enlightening and healing exercise in verbal processing.

Following the session, Caroline spoke privately to the therapist and thanked her through her tears for giving them "this wonderful gift." She said that while they never had difficulty expressing their feelings for each other, this was a new and beautiful way to pay tribute to their love. She asked the therapist to keep this song and sing it at Sam's funeral when that day comes.

### Final Thoughts

Sam and Caroline's version of *The 12th of Never* was sung about every third session and Sam reported that he listened to the CD the therapist made for him daily. They moved out of state shortly thereafter to spend Sam's final days in his daughter's home, with Caroline by his side.

This couple got under my skin more than other clients, which made self-care a must. It was an incredible honor to be a part of this man's life, providing comfort in his final months, and being witness to the extraordinary love he and his wife shared. They were an inspiration and a constant reminder of how rewarding music therapy work in hospice can be.

Human connections through music! Beautiful, isn't it? Let me tell you about one of the coolest little old ladies I've ever met and our work together ten years ago.

## CASE STUDY: MUSIC-MAKING, REMINISCENCE, AND INTIMATE VERBAL PROCESSING WITH A HOSPICE PATIENT

### Background Information

Jessie was a patient with Sunrise Health and Hospice from October 11, 2011 to December 28, 2012. She was admitted for hospice care with a diagnosis of "Unspecified Debility," which is a common diagnosis for terminally ill, frail older adults who are failing to thrive and do not exhibit a major system impairment that can be attributed to a single specific illness. In other words, the individual is dying of old age, slowly shutting down, and detaching from the world.

Jessie was referred for music therapy services by a nurse on October 26, 2011, two weeks after being admitted for hospice care. She was first visited by the music therapist on November 2, 2011 and was seen on a weekly basis for a little over a year. Patients are typically revoked from service after six months for "extended prognosis" unless they continue to show signs of decline. Jessie continued to qualify for services and her length of stay in this setting was not typical. In many cases, hospice patients in palliative care are only seen once or twice before passing. In a group home scenario, patients are visited on average three to twenty-four times. Jessie participated in more than fifty music therapy sessions.

Jessie was eighty-seven years old and lived in a group home in Gilbert, AZ with up to nine other residents. The total number of residents fluctuated, but five were consistent since Jessie moved in. She had a roommate, who was also a patient of Sunrise Health and Hospice. The residents shared meals at a large dining room table and spent most of their days sitting together in the family room watching television, without much interaction.

Despite being a smoker for the past sixty-one years, Jessie was not afflicted with lung cancer, emphysema, or any other related condition. She was non-ambulatory and used a wheelchair. She presented with lucidity, excellent reality orientation, moderate energy, minimal pain, and a bright affect until October of 2012, when she had visible shingles. She rapidly declined after that, as evidenced by frequent sleeping and drastically reduced responsiveness.

## Music Therapy Assessment

Sunrise Health and Hospice did not have a formal assessment procedure for ancillary therapies. Patients were typically referred for music therapy by a nurse or social worker with a brief description of the patient's needs and suggested goals for therapy. The music therapist reviewed the patient's medical records and consulted with the interdisciplinary team, but goals were determined upon informal assessment at the beginning of each session. Overall goals for Jessie, in the short and long term, included the following:

- Provide comfort
- Enhance quality of life
- Encourage social interaction
- Alleviate feelings of isolation or loneliness
- Promote sensory stimulation
- Distract from pain or discomfort
- Promote relaxation
- Elevate spirits
- Improve communication in dealing with difficult subjects
- Acknowledge and appropriately express emotions and spirituality

## Treatment Process

Because the music therapist had other Sunrise Health and Hospice patients at this group home, Jessie's sessions alternated weekly between 45-60-minute, 1:1 sessions and group sessions with some of the other residents. Individual sessions took place at bedside (when Jessie's roommate was not present) or privately in the living room. Group sessions were held in either the family room or living room. Nearly all sessions occurred around 10:30 a.m., before lunch.

The music therapist operated under an eclectic model, utilizing psychodynamic and holistic approaches to address Jessie's various needs and strengths. Music was frequently integrated with informal psychotherapy in 1:1 sessions. Group sessions primarily involved live music-making, musical reminiscence, and music-based discussions.

## Music-Making

Sing-alongs were the primary activity with groups, utilizing familiar music in such genres as oldies and standards, show tunes, patriotic songs, folk songs, country-western/cowboy songs (including Gene Autry, Roy Rogers, Harry McClintock, Johnny Cash, Kenny Rogers, Patsy Cline, Tammy Wynette, Charlie Daniels, and Willie Nelson), pop and rock songs (including Elvis, The Beatles, The Temptations, Everly Bros., Otis Redding, Johnny Nash, Simon & Garfunkel, John Denver, Van Morrison, and Roy Orbison), hymns/spirituals, and traditional holiday songs. Jessie expressed preferences in all these genres and was familiar with an impressive amount of repertoire. She quietly sang along or mouthed the words approximately 80% of the time during sing-alongs.

In both group and individual sessions, Jessie played a variety of instruments including egg shakers, maracas and other shakers, claves, cabasa, guiro, hand drum, tambourine, rhythm sticks, ocean drum, rainstick, jingle bells, glockenspiel, and tone chimes. Jessie played smaller instruments independently at about 95% rhythmic accuracy. In groups, she occasionally needed hand-over-hand assistance with larger instruments, which was often provided by a caregiver or visitor. The music therapist was able to provide that assistance in individual sessions.

Jessie demonstrated an infectious sense of humor and was often expressive without words. For example, in a group session where a fellow resident was boisterously singing off-key and several phrases behind, Jessie looked at the therapist with an expression of horror, simulated hanging herself, and smiled. Out of respect for the other residents, Jessie seemed to angle herself so that nobody else could see her and when the therapist smiled at her, she winked back.

During several individual sessions in late spring of 2012, the therapist developed an intervention to tap into Jessie's humor. Jessie often joked that she had been smoking for sixty-one years and wasn't about to quit now since it "hasn't killed me yet" (the group home allows her to go outside and smoke three cigarettes a day). The therapist introduced her to the Commander Cody version of *Smoke That Cigarette* on You Tube. Jessie laughed heartily and said, "Hey, that's a PRO-smoking song!" She said she liked the message, as well as the "cowboy-ish" style. The therapist returned for the following several individual sessions with the lyrics printed out in large font so that she and Jessie could sing the song together. After learning the basic structure of the song and solidifying the chorus, Jessie was able to add percussion. She usually tapped a tambourine to the beat through the verses and rattled it during rests in the chorus. Eventually, Jessie and the therapist sang the song together (Jessie sang the entire chorus, while the therapist sang the verses), as the therapist played guitar and Jessie played percussion. Bouts of laughter, smiles, and affectionate taps and slaps to the therapist were abundant by Jessie. Following are the lyrics to the song:

**SMOKE THAT CIGARETTE**

I'm a guy with a heart of gold, and the ways of a gentleman I've been told,

The kind of guy that'd never harm a flea.

But if me and a certain character met, the man who invented the cigarette,

I'd murder that son of a gun in the first degree!

Now it ain't 'cause I don't smoke myself, and I don't figure it'll hurt my health,

Been smokin' for twenty-five years, ain't dead yet.

Them nicotine slaves are all the same, at a pettin' party or a poker game,

Everything's gotta stop while you light up that cigarette.

**CHORUS:**

**Smoke, smoke, smoke that cigarette.**

**Puff, puff, puff it 'til you puff yourself to death.**

**Tell St. Peter at the Golden Gate that you hate to make him wait,**

**But you gotta have another cigarette.**

At a game of chance the other night, old Dame Fortune was doin' me right,

Kings and queens just kept on comin' 'round.

I played 'em low, I bet 'em high, but my bluff wasn't workin' on a certain guy,

Who kept on playin' and layin' his money down.

He'd raise me, I'd raise him, I sweated blood, you gotta sink or swim,

We finally called and then he raised the bet.

I said, "Aces—pow—now how 'bout you," he said, "I'll tell ya in a minute or two,

But right now I'm gonna have me another cigarette."

CHORUS

The other night I had a date with the cutest gal in the forty-eight states,

A regular uptown fancy kind of dame.

She said she loved me, and it seemed to me, things were goin' the way they're supposed to be,

Hand in hand we were strollin' down lover's lane.

She was oh so far from a cake of ice, our pettin' party was goin' real nice,

So help me Hanna, I'd have been there yet.

But I gave her a hug and a little squeeze, and she said, “Jimmy, ’scuze me please,

But right now I gotta have me another cigarette.”

CHORUS

Now life ain’t nothin’ but a poker game and no two hands are ever the same,

And I never met a winner that didn’t bet.

So if any of you folks are fixin’ to quit, I ain’t gonna criticize you one little bit,

Instead I’m gonna light me up another cigarette.

CHORUS

## Life Review and Reminiscence

Music can be a highly effective grounding element in structuring the processes of life review and reminiscence. Eric Erickson (1963) identified the final life stage task as resolving ego integrity versus ego despair. To do that, older adults need to look back on their lives and derive a sense of accomplishment and meaning. Recalling positive memories and identifying ways in which their lives were purposeful may contribute to their ability to achieve ego integrity.

Life review is structured around the developmental stages in a chronological review of one’s life. The role of the facilitator is to help individuals identify themes in their life histories, and to acknowledge how their experiences have influenced past and current behavior. The therapist can help evaluate and summarize the client’s responses, giving the individual a chance to integrate their memories into a life course perspective. The discussion may then move into what the individual hopes to accomplish in his or her remaining time, which can improve emotional well-being with resolution and acceptance. (McInnis-Dittrich, 2009)

Reminiscence is less structured and specifically designed to encourage older adults to remember and process positive memories. It does not focus on helping older adults resolve lifelong conflicts or attend to unfinished business, although this may come up. Reminiscence is intended to reinforce the belief that an individual is a worthwhile, valued human being, whereas life review attempts to achieve deeper insight. (McInnis-Dittrich, 2009)

From a life review and/or reminiscence perspective, many discussions took place in both individual and group music therapy sessions with Jessie, as directed and themed around the music. For example, singing *This Land is Your Land* inspired a conversation about favorite places to live or visit. Through these exercises, memories were shared about where the residents were born, where they lived and traveled, how many years they were married, how many children, grandchildren, and great grandchildren they have, what their occupations were, what military service they or loved ones were involved in, what cars they drove, what sports and/or arts they participated in, what they did for recreation, what their famous recipes were, what family holiday traditions they cherished, etc.

Following are some interesting facts about Jessie discovered through life review and reminiscence:

- Jessie has seven brothers and loved growing up as a tomboy.
- Jessie is from the Chicago area and spent most of her life in Illinois.
- Jessie graduated from high school, but did not attend college.
- Jessie played professional baseball (on one of the teams portrayed in the film, *A League of Their Own*) and had chronic knee problems after playing catcher for many years.
- Jessie spent thirty-one years in the Air Force as a funds manager.

- Jessie was never married and has no children.
- Jessie is Christian, but did not practice regularly after leaving her family's home.
- Jessie's favorite treat is Nutter Butter cookies!

## Intimate Sharing and Processing

Music therapy can help the terminally ill in two specific ways. First, it can be used to accomplish traditional therapeutic or clinical goals, such as reduction of anxiety, distraction from pain, and strengthening of self-concept. Second, music can be a source of deep and meaningful interaction between patients and families, patients and patients, and in this case, patients and the therapist. (Martin, 1991)

Jessie was more forthcoming about her history during individual sessions. It didn't take long for a strong rapport to develop between Jessie and the therapist. Trust was well-established after only a few sessions, but it took ten months before Jessie made a big revelation.

Jessie had often spoken fondly of her best friend of sixty-two years, Joanie (who is also Jessie's power of attorney and former caregiver). The therapist met Joanie on a few occasions when she happened to be visiting during the music therapy session. She joined a couple group sessions and actively participated. Her camaraderie and long-standing relationship with Jessie were evident through their eye contact, facial expressions, and mutual touch.

In a number of individual sessions, Jessie had given the therapist clues to her sexuality and her relationship with Joanie without admitting anything outright. The therapist sensed that Jessie wanted to share a secret—needed to share a secret. After dancing around the subject in the context of a discussion about love and marriage, while singing several love songs, the therapist asked Jessie if there's something she wants to tell the therapist. Jessie said, "I think you already know. Can you guess?" The therapist responded by saying, "Just so there's no confusion, why don't you tell me exactly what it is you want me to know. Remember, anything you tell me is in complete confidence and I will not judge you." Jessie took a deep breath and said, "I'm a lesbian." The therapist nodded and revealed no emotion. Jessie asked, "Do you think I'm disgusting?" To this, the therapist was surprised and said, "I have absolutely no problem with your sexuality. I work in the arts, after all!" Jessie laughed. The therapist asked why Jessie used the word disgusting. Jessie said she has never told anyone in her entire life except for a very select few, mainly because she feared that people would think she's disgusting. She explained that she grew up in a devoutly Christian family and many of her relatives were fundamentally and outspokenly against homosexuality.

This discussion evolved into a lengthy verbal processing exercise that had Jessie in tears. She told the therapist these were tears of joy and relief, and even if she never reveals her secret to anyone else, she feels tremendous gratitude to the therapist for her willingness to listen without judgment. This led to some chanting and simple singing of mantras created by both Jessie and the therapist, including "Love who you love," "I am who I am," "I've been blessed with love in my life," and "Don't judge me—I'm wonderful!"

Jessie declined further exploration and expression in this subject area and chose not to involve Joanie in an individual session, which the therapist respected. Jessie also declined the therapist's inquiry into whether Jessie would like to be referred to a counselor. She said, "I have you! I don't want to talk to someone new." Jessie and the therapist did not discuss her sexuality in detail thereafter, but every now and then, when there was a reference made to a spouse or partner, Jessie met the therapist's eye with a smile or a wink. The therapist let Jessie take the lead in this area and if the subject came up again, would support her through music and talk therapy.

## Approaching the End

With Jessie's decline, there was a change in focus for therapy to more comfort care. At this point, goals primarily addressed distraction from pain and discomfort, promoting relaxation, and enhancing quality of life. Interventions included singing of more sedative oldies/standards and hymns, Music Assisted Relaxation (MAR), imagery, playing of soft guitar, Native American flute, and ocean drum, vocalizing, and humming. Jessie still responded by alternating between active and passive listening (often with eyes closed), occasionally singing quietly and contributing to discussions, making eye contact and smiling or nodding at the therapist, reaching out for the therapist and squeezing her hand, and making a visible effort to remain engaged. Sessions were being cut shorter and shorter as Jessie either fell asleep or appeared too fatigued to actively participate. The therapist on several occasions reminded Jessie that she will not be insulted if Jessie falls asleep and not to fight it.

Jessie's regression over the next several weeks was rapid and uneventful. She passed peacefully in her sleep, in her bed at the group home, a few days after Christmas on December 28, 2012.

## Discussion And Conclusions

Music therapy has tremendous benefits in end-of-life care. Some of the interventions described here come from a psychotherapy perspective and it is strongly recommended that practitioners in this environment participate in advanced training, particularly in counseling. Intuition, reflective listening, advanced verbal response skills, and the ability to implement affective, cognitive, and behavioral strategies or any combination thereof (Okun, 2002) are paramount to progress. Knowledge of death and dying, as well as excellent, flexible musicianship are of equal importance.

In addition to Jessie's brave revelation and subsequent self-acceptance, she was able to review her life through her accomplishments and relationships. Live music-making, the use of humor, and life review and reminiscence interventions achieved many of the goals identified for Jessie, and she seemed to be in a place of resolution and peace in her final days.

Honoring Jessie's extensive preferences for music likely contributed to the rapport established between her and the therapist. This is essential in any music therapy relationship. In addition, the ability to administer an immediate assessment is critical for effective treatment of presenting needs.

In closing, it is recommended that music therapists working in the hospice environment acknowledge the emotional challenges involved in this work. To be present for patients and work in the moment, music therapists must allow themselves time to process, grieve, and recharge. Ethical issues of boundaries and countertransference must be considered and confronted. If the music therapist engages in self-care, burnout and breakdown are far less likely.

Music therapy in hospice is substantial but gratifying work. It takes a lot of heart, guts, and mindfulness. It isn't always pretty. It isn't always easy. But there is great honor and dignity behind improving the quality of life for someone approaching death.

I frequently pull songwriting out of my arsenal for psychosocial work. Trevor was a forty-something hospice patient who was dying of AIDS. I visited him twice. The first time, we wrote the following song together:

**WHEN THAT DAY COMES**

Mom, you were always so accepting.

Dad, I know it's hard for you sometimes.

I've been so truly blessed to have my family and my friends.

Thanks for always being so kind.

Rollie, I remember men I met you.

You absolutely blew me away.

I wouldn't change a thing despite the suffering and the pain.

I really wish I knew just what to say.

**CHORUS:**

**I'm going on a brand new adventure.**

**For me, the journey's just begun.**

**I know someday we'll all be back together.**

**Imagine all the joy when that day comes.**

Everybody feels that time is stolen.

Please believe I did the best I could.

I hope you know that if there was a way to ease your pain,

With everything I am, I surely would.

CHORUS x2

Imagine all the love when that day comes.

For the second visit (he passed a couple days later), I brought Trevor a CD recording of the song, along with notated sheet music. He was profoundly grateful to have something to leave behind for his loved ones. Something they could touch and hear...his tender words of gratitude.

I apologize for all the death and dying, but these stories are so much more illustrative of music therapy than a bunch of indecipherable statistics. Last one, I promise. While completing my undergraduate degree in music therapy, I taught music at a K-8 private school. We lost one of our fourth-grade students, Jarrod, in a tragic skiing accident. As part of the grieving process, I facilitated a songwriting exercise with Jarrod's class to assist the students in identifying and expressing their emotions of sadness, confusion, disbelief, and anger. We performed the song for Jarrod's parents and lovingly presented them with the lyrics in Jarrod's honor.

## JARROD'S SONG

By the Fourth Graders of PARDES Jewish Day School

Jarrod was a really, really close friend.

We'd always talk about the newest trends.

We wish you could come back, so we could spend more time with you.

We never thought that it could ever end.

It would be too painful to forget you.

Bet we couldn't, even if we tried.

We'll make your mother smile, and your brother for a while.

It hurts so much; we wish you hadn't died.

**CHORUS:**

**He always had a great imagination.**

**He loved sports, the color orange, too.**

**A math whiz with amazing concentration,**

**And tomatoes were his very favorite food.**

Jarrod, wow, we really can't believe it.

You were always such a funny kid.

So thoughtful, energetic, creative, and friendly,

Smart and kind with everything you did.

Hard-working and cheerful, that describes you.

Caring, helpful, always having fun.

A great friend and student, you were focused and on-track.

Whenever someone needed you, you'd come.

CHORUS

We thought you could've stayed; you shouldn't be gone.

It's such a shame you had to disappear.

Couldn't you stay longer, we're so sad you had to go.

Don't you know your name is all we hear?

His friendship was better than a hundred dollars.

Jarrod could make anybody smile.

That's just who he was, we'll see you someday again with God.

Until then, he'll be watching over Kyle.

CHORUS

We'll pray for you forever, all together.

We believe in you and we'll be strong.

Why did you have to go, no one so young deserves to die,

Especially when you did nothing wrong.

We were friends, we liked to be together.

We were playing not so long ago.

Well miss you, that's for sure, if only they found a cure.

It's not fair that these things happen, who can know?

CHORUS

A really awesome dude, that was J-Rod.

Football was his thing, the Giants rule!

When we were feeling sad, you were the one to cheer us up.

You never got mad and that's so cool.

Why did you have to go so early?

Why'd you have to leave us in mid-stride?

We never will forget you, every night our tears will fall,

But you'll always be with us inside.

CHORUS

You'll have a good time with God and all the angels.

It's like a new beginning for you.

Your friends are missing you so badly, but we'll help your family gladly.

You'll never leave our hearts; you know it's true.

CHORUS

We're all so sorry that this had to happen.

We hope you knew how much we loved you.

Death is never the end for those who remain. Our memories are rich treasures, often associated with music. Let's celebrate all those we love, of this earth and beyond. Make a list of the most prominent people in your life and assign them a song. Don't forget a song for yourself!

# X. THERE'S A SONG FOR THAT OCCASION

*"It's your thing. Do what you wanna do." —Isley Brothers*

Among its many other superpowers, music reflects the values and behaviors of a given culture. In addition to expressing social norms, music has always been used to validate social institutions and religious rituals. Consider the times you sang the national anthem or your school fight song. Have you ever joined in singing *The Battle Hymn of the Republic* or *Amazing Grace* at a political or religious event to strengthen your resolve? Music is the bearer of cultural beliefs shared among members of the community and transmitted from one generation to the next.

Research suggests that socioeconomic status can affect our cultural perspectives and preferences. Those with higher income and advanced formal education have been linked to opera and symphonic works more so than blue-collar workers. Cultural context is unequivocally relevant when using music toward a therapeutic purpose. Social integration is a common objective of music therapy and is likely a reason for your own musical immersion.

I mentioned the functional uses of music back in the book's introduction. Music can function effectively for multiple therapeutic purposes in its many societal uses. A.P. Merriam (1964) outlined the following ten functions of music in society:

1. Physical response
2. Communication
3. Emotional expression
4. Symbolic representation
5. Enforcement of conformity to social norms
6. Validation of social institutions and religious rituals
7. Contribution to the continuity and stability of culture
8. Contribution to the integration of society
9. Aesthetic enjoyment
10. Entertainment

In a music therapy context, music can also function as a carrier of information, a form of reinforcement, a background for learning, a physical structure for a learning activity, and a reflection of skills or processes learned. Like a music experience, an occasion or event can provide all kinds of interpersonal opportunities.

Songs contribute to how one perceives their group within social constructs. Music for social bonding is related to shared preferences and similar values between individuals and groups. The blues, for example, have alone had a tremendous influence in the United States and abroad, as it balances a celebration of love and sex with dark humor and wry commentary about the human condition. Hearing a blues song can make one feel acknowledged and understood. Writing and singing a blues song can give a voice to emotions ranging from deep sorrow to bitter disappointment to spirited joy. Blues songs have illustrated how music can bind together, organize, and distinguish one group from another, while reinforcing defining principles of what is important in life (Norton, 2016). Slaves, soldiers, prisoners. Imagine how their experiences would have been shaped without music.

Music often marks important life occasions. We use music to create memories about these events. Music supports and even defines meeting places where social networks are established and people feel a sense of belonging. What songs do you associate with specific occasions/events?

Beginning with the nuptials, I have sung some of these, heard some of these, and cringed over some of these songs associated with weddings and wedding receptions:

- *All I Ask of You*, from *Phantom of the Opera*
- *All of Me*, John Legend
- *Another One Bites the Dust*, Queen (c'mon, that's funny)
- *A Thousand Years*, Christina Perri
- *Butterfly Kisses*, Bob Carlisle
- *Celebration*, Kool & The Gang
- (The Effing) *Chicken Dance*
- *Evergreen*, Barbra Streisand
- *Every Breath You Take*, The Police (stalker much?)
- *Have I Told You Lately*, Van Morrison/Rod Stewart
- *I Cross My Heart*, George Strait
- *I Swear*, John Michael Montgomery
- *Late in the Evening*, Paul Simon (we conga lined through the ballroom kitchen to a surprised and amused staff at my ludicrously fun wedding!)
- *One Hand One Heart*, from *West Side Story*
- *Right Down the Line*, Gerry Rafferty

- *Shallow*, Lady Gaga
- *Single Ladies*, Beyoncé
- *The Way You Look Tonight*, Frank Sinatra
- *Time After Time*, Cyndi Lauper
- *To Make You Feel My Love*, Bob Dylan
- *We Are Family*, Sister Sledge

What songs come to mind for you in relation to the following occasions?

- Anniversaries
- Back to school/End of school
- Births
- Birthdays
- Celebrations
- Congratulations
- Cultural events
- First dances
- Funerals
- Graduations
- Holidays…New Years, Valentine's Day, Easter, Passover, Memorial Day, Fourth of July, Labor Day, Halloween, Veteran's Day, Thanksgiving, Hanukkah, Christmas
- Religious events
- Rites of passage (confirmation, bar/bat mitzvah, quinceañera, etc.)
- Retirement

Do you have loads of songs, artists, and genres bouncing around between your ears? Important occasions deserve good music! And that music immeasurably reinforces memories built at special occasions.

The use of music, and music therapy, can serve society's need for a more humanized concept of health, wellness, identity, and community. Music provides a sense of group belonging in communal spaces. Music is so deeply embedded in our world that it has the power to influence cultural and social transformation. We establish a musical identity much the same way we create personal and social identities. A collective musical experience is the mutual sharing of socially and culturally constructed intentions. Plus, it's really, really fun.

I end this section with a parody my band wrote and performed at a Friends for Life Animal Shelter fundraiser event a few decades ago. Enjoy SRB's puppy verse to Steve Miller Band's *The Joker*:

Canines always barkin' at me, baby
Nippin' sideways at my heels
But unconditional love is my reward
As long as I remember your meals

Dig in the trash and chew on my shoes
Roll in the dirt right after a bath
Slobber flyin', slobber flyin', slobber flyin', slobber flyin'
Ooo, your landmines are in my path

I'm a shepherd, I'm a beagle, I'm a mastiff, and I'm a pit bull
I French poodle all night long
I'm a schnauzer, I'm a dachshund, part pug and greyhound
I chase pussies just for fun
Ooo, ooo, (howl)

# XI. VERSE-CHORUS-VERSE-CHORUS-BRIDGE-CHORUS-CHORUS

*"For those about to rock, we salute you." —AC/DC*

Have any of these stories touched your heart or sparked your imagination? Have I provided enough empirical evidence to convince any remaining skeptics out there that music can positively impact your life? (Music haters probably hate chocolate too. Miscreants.)

In this chapter, I invite you to find ways to purposefully incorporate more music into your life. I also encourage you to use music with loved ones. How can you utilize music to connect with others? How can you use music to help others learn, function, cope, or remember? It's time to find your songs. To use your songs. The music and lyrics that define you and your experiences.

You can use music for meaningful interactions with others, even if you have no musical background. Whether you've never touched an instrument, sing only in the car (because we're all invisible in our cars), or attend the symphony every Friday night, you can translate your love of music into a tool for connection, communication, and expression. You may not be qualified to facilitate formal music therapy, but you can certainly use music therapeutically with others and for yourself. Be cautioned, however, that if your experiences delve into beyond-the-surface medical or psychological territory, it is your ethical human responsibility to reach out to a professional—a doctor, nurse, psychiatrist, counselor, social worker, physical therapist, occupational therapist, speech language pathologist, music therapist, art therapist, recreation therapist, dance/movement therapist, clergy, or whatever modality requires licensing or board-certification (and maintenance). Do not attempt to "treat" yourself or another. Unless you yourself are a health practitioner, you have no scope of practice. With lack of education and training, you could inadvertently cause damage. Physicians take the Hippocratic Oath. Those of us in helping fields adopt the same philosophy to practice non-maleficence. (Stepping off soap box.)

So let's do this. Are you a music consumer or a music creator? Both? Create your fate and make it happen! Start wherever you're least intimidated, play to your strengths, and just go for it. You already learned about drumming and rhythm in Chapter 5. Get your hands on a drum you will love (and play). West Music has the best prices I've found for just about any instrument you can think of. My favorite finds—and amazing deals—were on eBay. If you see an instrument you like at an art festival or similar event, buy it immediately or you'll have non-buyer's remorse. Or if you decide to wait and buy it on the way out, you'll never find it again.

You could also make your own drum or other hand-percussion instruments. Try these instrument recipes:

- Drums...Use empty coffee cans, candy tins, large margarine tubs, etc. Keep the plastic lid, as this is where you will strike your drum. Cover with construction paper, aluminum foil, tissue paper, etc. and decorate. Also, try using a metal bowl covered with a stretched balloon.

- Shakers…Use empty soda cans, plastic bottles, tennis ball packaging tubes, Pringles containers, Tupperware, etc., and fill with dry beans, dry rice, dry pasta, pebbles, gravel, or paper clips. Seal well with heavy-duty tape. Cover with construction paper, wrapping paper, aluminum foil, or tissue paper and decorate with crayons, marker, paint, stickers, etc. You can also fill plastic Easter eggs with dry rice and glue them closed to create egg shakers. (When all else fails, shake a pill bottle or a set of keys!)
- Jingle bells…Sew individual bells onto an elastic band (scrunchies work well) to be worn on the wrist or ankle.
- Rainsticks…

  *Materials Needed:*

  Paper towel or wrapping paper roll

  Chicken wire

  Rice (uncooked)

  Construction paper, wrapping paper, cardboard pieces

  Heavy duty tape

  Paint, markers, stickers, etc. for decorating

  *Procedure:*

  1. Measure and cut the appropriate size of chicken wire. Roll the chicken wire compactly so that it will fit into the paper towel or wrapping paper roll.
  2. Cover one end of the roll with a square of construction paper or round piece of cardboard. Fold it around the sides of the roll and tape it down securely. Also tape across the covered end for extra durability.
  3. Fill the roll with uncooked rice about 1/3 full.

4. Cover the other end of the roll in the same manner as instructed in step 2.
5. Cover the entire roll with construction paper or wrapping paper, hiding the tape.
6. Decorate.

Pretty easy so far, yes? How about musical games? Break out the Encore board game or trivia cards. Endless music game apps are waiting to be downloaded. Create bingo cards and corresponding playlists for music genres or artists or whatever you come up with. Make a Musical Jeopardy board and write questions in such groupings as genres, decades, soundtracks, Disney, instruments, composers, Grammys, Tonys, etc. I use the categories game a lot as an icebreaker with my behavioral health groups (this a great drinking game too, but I don't mention that!). I do this a couple ways. First, I pick a category, such as bands, and the group goes through the alphabet, naming a band for each letter (Aerosmith, Beatles, CCR…). Second, pick a category and go around in a circle, singing (or saying/chanting) songs with the category in the title or lyrics. Popular song categories are colors (*Blue Suede Shoes*, *Purple Rain*, etc.), geographic locations (*California Dreamin'*, *Please Come to Boston*, etc.), and weather (*Come Rain or Come Shine*, *Thunder*, etc.). A single word can also be a category: love, sun, baby, etc. We could do this for hours.

Perhaps your loved one is recovering from a stroke and struggling with speech and movement. Encourage singing and chanting, as well as whistling and blowing, to strengthen the mechanism and musculature of both speech and singing. Encourage your loved one to blow into whistles, recorders/flutes, and harmonicas. Get silly with a kazoo—another rehabilitation tool. Carefully chosen music can also assist in re-establishing walking gait. Make sure tempo starts slow and remains consistent.

You may recall some of the hospice case studies I shared in Chapter 9, where I depicted how music can assist in the loss of brain function (e.g., Alzheimer's, dementia, schizophrenia, etc.). You can facilitate life review and reminiscence through music with elderly loved ones, especially toward the end of life. The geriatric cohort is the greatest generation. Their stories are so important! Ask about their lives. Learn the little details. Pick a song, an artist, or a movie from their time to help generate memories. Ask questions like, "How old were you when you saw that movie? Where did you see it? Who were you with? Who starred in the movie? What music do you remember from it?"

Create a lifeline album with and for your loved one, using songs that represent milestones or favorite songs by decades. Take Frank Sinatra's *It Was a Very Good Year* and create a personal narrative. Was seventeen a good year? Why? How about twenty-one? What do you remember about thirty-five? And so on.

Sing or listen to songs together and use specific lyric content to promote discussion. After singing or listening to *I've Been Workin' on the Railroad*, ask your loved one about their career, what jobs they had/liked/disliked, etc. After singing or listening to *New York, New York*, ask your loved one where they have traveled, what their favorite/least favorite trip was, etc. With *Que Sera Sera*, ask about relationships, boyfriends/girlfriends, family, children, grandchildren, etc. Get creative and always honor your loved one's preferences. In other words, don't traumatize Great Aunt Mildred with Pantera when you know Tony Bennett is her jam.

Listening and observing are the best things you can do during these interactions. Older people—especially the curmudgeons—have wise, insightful, and brilliantly hilarious advice to impart ("Marriage is for suckers," "Always eat dessert first"). They can also be highly entertaining, God bless 'em, like the time an older woman in a group home stood up and requested assistance to the bathroom. While she waited for the caregiver, a firm round poop fell out of her pants and rolled across the floor. I was leading the group in *Ain't She Sweet* (the aroma was not). Yes, that association is with me forever. I once observed another woman in hospice care being escorted to the bathroom who farted in perfect rhythm with each step. I will never unsee the twig and berries of exposed ninety-year-old men. These moments are all connected to a song!

If you're not singing your own praises yet, I hope you're at least singing—the very first form of music. The human body is the instrument and vessel of vocal music. Your voice was the first musical instrument you ever played. It is uniquely yours. An identifier—an indicator of individuality. Humans are designed as resonating, acoustic, musical instruments. Plus, a voice is a lot easier to schlep than a tuba.

Ongoing research connects brain function, behavior, and emotions to music, and more specifically, to the singing voice. I personally believe everyone should sing. Not necessarily on stage. But for whatever you need addressed. Sing to release and rejoice. To uncover and unite.

### Singing offers multiple benefits and can:

- lower stress levels
- strengthen the immune system
- increase pain threshold
- improve snoring
- improve lung function/respiration
- help develop a sense of belonging and connection
- enhance memory
- alleviate grief
- improve mental health and mood
- improve speaking abilities
- decrease depression through the release of endorphins
- improve mental alertness

The voice is a vital source of connection to oneself. When people sing, they are intimately connected to their breath, bodies, and emotional lives. The voice is a bridge that connects mind and body, thinking and feeling. Singing is a direct way to express intense emotions. It is also a way to transcend everyday reality and connect with the transpersonal, spiritual dimensions of life.

Whether you consider yourself a singer or not, SING! Wherever, whenever, with whomever. Another word of caution, though (five, actually). Take care of your voice! My dad (remember, the voice professor?) and I compiled a worksheet on vocal care that I repeatedly reviewed with my practicum students. These exercises and techniques are also recommended if you speak a lot during the day. Suggestions:

- ALWAYS warm up first thing in the morning. The voice is a muscle. Just as you would stretch your legs before you run to avoid an injury, you must do the same for your voice! Start light and do some simple vocalizations in the shower or in the car:

1. Humming
   a. Slide back and forth from 5-1 (e.g., G-C)
   b. Slide a descending octave
2. Lip trills and sirens (up and down yawn sighs)
   c. Staccato—then legato 1-3-5-3-1 (e.g., C-E-G-E-C)
   d. Legato 1-3-5-8-5-3-1 (e.g., C-E-G-C-G-E-C)
3. Vs (slide up and down an octave)

Do not overdo these exercises. A few repetitions now, and again later, will suffice.

- Breathe low by releasing the stomach/abdominal area and naturally expanding. Do not collapse/sink at the beginning of a phrase.
- Posture is very important—soft. long neck (free neck), back lengthened and widened, rib cage out during whole phrases, head held level and balanced over the torso, loose jaw, and unlocked knees.
- To release stress and tension, do the "ragdoll"—bend over toward the floor with knees unlocked. Let everything "flop" toward the floor and just let it all go. Do this for about 10-15 seconds and then rise back up slowly.
- Try to vary your vocal techniques and sing in several styles (classical, pop, blues, etc.). Flip-flopping from one genre to another can be challenging, but the more you practice, the easier it will become.
- Also work on expanding your range. First sopranos are highly unlikely to sing in their most comfortable range with others. Oftentimes, you can sing an octave above, but for pitch matching purposes, you need to hit those lower notes. Singing in more of the rock and pop styles and will help you achieve this. So will the warm-ups, which stretch the muscle. Men: It is helpful for young male voices to use their falsetto. With strengthening over time, that voice can begin to add some of the lower voice "weight" and develop a true head voice. Like female singers, the untrained male tends to push the chest voice way too high.
- Drink a lot of water throughout the day, preferably at room temperature.
- Avoid smoking and caffeine in tea, soda, and coffee, as these tend to limit needed moisture at the vocal folds. Also limit alcohol consumption. (Do as I say, not as I do!)

- Avoid constantly speaking in the lower range of your voice. Think British!

Now that you know how to sing like a pro, let's talk songwriting. Do not be intimidated by that word! KEEP. IT. SIMPLE. If you are a musician and you know how to read notation and/or tablature, this will be fairly easy. I use the guitar as my primary instrument for accompaniment and I play rhythmic chord progressions. I'm a strummer, not a shredder. No need for virtuosity. Same goes for piano, ukulele, or whatever you'd like to use as your support instrument. If you can play four chords (e.g., G, E minor, C, and D on guitar or C, A minor, F, and G on piano or ukulele), you can play about 90% of popular music (rock, pop, country, blues, folk, hymns, etc.). Just learn a few basics so that you can support yourself singing. Or don't use any accompaniment at all outside of simple percussion or clapping. And there's no shame in singing a cappella.

There are no formal rules for songwriting. Start with lyrics or start with melody and musical content—whichever comes more naturally. Consider common formats for songs. Introduction, verses, choruses, maybe a bridge. A lot of songs follow the I-IV-V7-I format, such as C-F-G7-C or G-C-D7-G. You can experiment and elaborate with this progression and your ear may be of great assistance, as you hear familiar patterns and begin to expect changes and resolutions.

Verse-chorus-verse-chorus-bridge-chorus-chorus is a common song structure. Think of it as telling a story. Verse one introduces the story, sets it up, draws the listener in. The chorus is the main theme of the song. Verse two yanks you further into the bigger picture. The chorus reminds you there's a point to all of this. The bridge then takes the listener in a slightly different direction with a tangent, a twist, a solution…and then it returns to a double chorus to tie it all up in a neat little bow ending. The lyrics are your story, your message, your dilemma, your purge.

Do your lyrics have to rhyme? Heck, no! Use rhyming words if they work, but this is completely up to you. It's all part of the process, which involves creating melody, chords, rhythm, and lyrics. You will most likely choose a song in quadruple or triple meter (e.g., 4/4 or 3/4 time signatures) but with more advanced musical skills, you can make things more challenging. Avoid complexity in rhythms as well as melodies so you don't get discouraged.

There are a few schools of songwriting that I use in my practice and just for fun. A song parody is where you take an existing song and change the words. I also use a fill-in-the-blank system to create parodies with clients. My most frequently used and most successful form of songwriting is the twelve-bar blues. I share multiple examples of this in the following pages. The standard progression goes like this:

| | |
|---|---|
| I-I-I-I | (E-E-E-E) |
| IV-IV-I-I | (A-A-E-E) |
| V7-IV-I-V7 | (B7-A-E-B7) |

Here's a spicier version:

| | |
|---|---|
| I-I-I-I7 | (E-E-E-E7) |
| IV7-IV7-I-I | (A7-A7-E-E) |
| V7-IV7-I-V7 | (B7-A7-E-B7) |

Starting from scratch requires more work and more experience, but you may find a nice chord progression that you can use as a template for writing songs. Use repeated ideas and patterns, both lyrically and musically. Rhythmically and melodically emphasize important words and phrases. If you can't carry a tune in a bucket, try rapping it.

Songwriting is a useful tool for learning and self-expression, both by yourself and with others. What is your starting point going to be? What kind of structure are you going to use? Do you want to probe into deeper content and lyrics? This is your rodeo, so don't think too much and just have fun!

I have songs to share with you! The following tunes were written with and by clients and patients—real people with varying levels of musical experience. I'll begin with some of those twelve-bar blues creations.

One of my very favorite client groups is Cortney's Place in Scottsdale, AZ. It's a mixed bag of developmental and medical diagnoses, personalities, and preferences. Every one of these special individuals is very near and dear to my heart. On a toasty day in May, a discussion about the weather organically ensued as we were approaching the dreaded Arizona summer. The following song was written on the spot:

**THE TOO-HOT BLUES**

The temperature is rising way too fast for me

The snakes are comin' out just like the scorpions and the bees

I don't want to get poisoned or stung

Triple digit heat is just plain wrong

I got the too-hot blues, and that is not good news

I'm tired, I have no energy, hope I don't get heat rash

By the time I get home, I'll just have to crash

I'm sweatin' like a pig and that's no fun

Black wheelchairs get as hot as the sun

I got the too-hot blues, and that is not good news

Better stay inside and enjoy the nice A/C

Peeling, sunburned skin and heatstroke's not for me

It's better in the shade or I can get in the pool

I drink a lot of water to keep me cool

I got the too-hot blues, and that is not good news

The next blues song was written with a junior high school group in a self-contained classroom of kids with emotional and behavioral disorders in Cave Creek, AZ. They were venting about their limitations and reputations, which resulted in a song. PLC is an acronym for their program, but I cannot for the life of me remember what it stands for.

**THE PLC BLUES**

Can't switch classes, I'm stuck in the same old room
I can't see my friends and I have to live with this 'til June
I feel like the teachers are really unfair
I don't think I'll ever get to run for mayor
I got the PLC blues
I can't even break in my shoes

People make fun of us when we walk through the halls
Sometimes I feel like I want to punch through the walls
They strap us to the seat on the special ed bus
We're labeled as retarded, but that's just not us
I got the PLC blues
But this is not what I would choose

I find working with adolescents to be highly challenging, but super fun. These two nuggets came from an adolescent group at the behavioral health hospital I work for in Tempe, AZ:

**GET ME OUTA HERE BLUES**

Woke up this mornin', I was feelin' cranky
Angsty, lazy, irritated, and downright angry

Gonna hit the gym to relieve my stress

Hope it'll help 'cuz I'm kind of a mess

I got the wanna-go-home blues

Like my mind, I'm ready to cruise

Woke up this mornin', I was feelin' pissed

People say unnecessary things, makes me ball up my fist

In the past, I'd get aggressive and beat someone's ass

But now I go outside and just lay in the grass

I got the annoying people blues

'Cause somebody stole my shoes

Several years ago, I established a weekly music therapy group of teen boys with Aspergers (more commonly known today as High Functioning Autism [HFA]) to promote social interaction, emotional expression, and self-esteem building. They lived in different parts of the metropolitan Phoenix area and did not know each other outside the group, but became fast friends who validated and supported each other. This little ditty emerged out of a discussion about bullying and was accompanied with piano.

**THE MEAN PEOPLE BLUES**

(Alan's verse)

I was at my locker

Got punched in the face

Had a black eye for two weeks

It was all a big disgrace

I got the blues

The mean people blues

I think these people are really bad news

I got the mean people blues

(Ricky's verse)

A bully fifth grader

Got me with a burning punch

I got my revenge later

I chased him around a whole bunch

I got the blues

The mean people blues

I think these people are really bad news

I got the mean people blues

(Daniel's verse)

I was playing NUTZO

Got slapped in the eye

But my little sister,

She made me want to cry

I got the blues

The mean people blues

I think these people are really bad news

I got the mean people blues

(Jeff's verse)

Was leaving school in fourth grade

A bully snatched my hat

He held it up over my head

Can you imagine that?

I got the blues

The mean people blues

I think these people are really bad news

I got the mean people blues

(Vincent's verse)

A boy named Tyler,

He called me dumb

He was a great big liar

I won't let him make me feel bummed

I got the blues

The mean people blues

I think these people are really bad news

I got the mean people blues

While on the oncology ward of Phoenix Children's Hospital, I worked for several weeks with an eleven-year-old insightful young man. Doug was an old soul, wise far beyond his years. I facilitated a lyric analysis of Jim Croce's *Time in a Bottle*, which led to Doug's revelation that if it is indeed his time, he is ready to go; however, he was very concerned about his parents and their grief. Following some heavy verbal processing, we transitioned into a blues songwriting intervention about one of Doug's recent procedures. We brainstormed and laughed. We lifted the heavy.

**DOUG'S HOSPITAL BLUES**

I had no food for five long, awful days

The hunger pains and watching Mom eat put me in a haze

I just had breakfast and I'm hungry again

Bread and jello didn't quite cut it then

I got the hospital hunger blues

But my Power Aide is helping me cruise

I was in isolation for a few weeks

No visitors, I was bored and lonely—that just stinks!

Need someone to talk to, YouTube isn't a friend

But my I.V. is, morphine brings the pain to an end.

The test results were negative—yes!

Now my visitors are back, that's the best!

A private client of mine, August, had a fascinating brain and was challenged by schizoaffective disorder. August was in his fifties, sedentary and overweight. He was also a fantastic Broadway singer, a loving friend, and a goofball. He frequently mused about his size and his constant struggle to eat healthy and get moving. The final blues example I want to share with you is from August's ponderings about the bulge battle.

**THE WEIGHT LOSS BLUES**

A little voice says, "Don't eat it"

Another says, "Just take one bite"

But sometimes I mess up

Once in a while that's alright

I got the blues

The weight loss blues

A salad is probably the thing I should choose

I got the weight loss blues

Got no one to talk to

When it's late at night

It makes me want to gorge

Will I ever win this fight?

I got the blues

The weight loss blues

A salad is probably the thing I should choose

I got the weight loss blues

I explained song parodies a few pages back. If the prospect of songwriting is still daunting, parodies are a great place to start. Take any song you know and simply write new lyrics. Be silly. Be profound. Try different moods. I repeat: keep it simple.

The next two song parodies were also written on the oncology unit of Phoenix Children's Hospital:

To the tune of *You Are My Sunshine*

You are my chemo, my only chemo

You make me nauseous and sleep all day

My hair is thinning, although I need you

Please don't take my chemo away

To the tune of *My Bonnie*

I'm nauseous, I just lost my breakfast

I need help when I have to pee

My hair's gone, I'm sick of these do-rags

Oh, bring back my morphine to me

Bring back, bring back, oh, bring back my morphine to me, to me

Bring back, bring back, oh, bring back my morphine to me

My energy's gone, I'm lethargic

I'm so sick of watching TV

I don't know how I got so skinny

Oh, bring back my morphine to me

Bring back, bring back, oh, bring back my morphine to me, to me

Bring back, bring back, oh, bring back my morphine to me

Here's another one from the Cave Creek junior high group. We wrote a song for Thanksgiving to practice mindfulness and gratitude:

To the tune of John Denver's *Leavin' on a Jet Plane*:

I go to the movies and eat popcorn

I hike in the mountains; I hope there's no storm

Kickball, soccer, I love all these sports

I love watching football on Thanksgiving day

When the weather's nice, I go out to play

Watch the news and take a nap, relax

Sister and brothers, I sure love my mom and dad

So many great things in my life

I'm thankful for my family

I have a roof above my head

Turkey at the feast makes me smile

My friends are cool, I can go to school

When it's hot outside, I can jump in the pool

My pets, they love me unconditionally

The clothes on my back keep me warm and dry

I can have big dreams like wanting to fly

I know that I can always fall back on me

'Cause I have activities, music and skateboarding

Acting, movies, and MySpace too

I'm thankful for my family

I have a roof above my head

My belly's always full

Speaking of gratitude, I facilitated groups on Thanksgiving day 2020 at the psych hospital. While patients made paper flowers, writing things they're grateful for on the petals, I surreptitiously constructed their words into a parody of *My Favorite Things* from *The Sound of Music*:

**MY GRATITUDE THINGS**

(Adolescents)

Family, veggie straws, crystals, and women

Meds, when they're working, and all of my friends

Sweaters and music and crafting and games

These are a few of my gratitude things

A good economy, plenty of money

Spotify, nature, and sweet dogs and cats

School and clothing and food and art

These are a few of my gratitude things

Toxic relationships and addiction

When I'm feeling sad

I simply remember my gratitude things

And then I don't feel so bad

(Adults)

Family and friends, love, my faith, and trust

Music and dancing and going to church

Sleeping and pets, health, and video games

These are a few of my gratitude things

Getting my help at 'Recovery Mountain'

Privacy, new job, and increasing confidence

My home, new acquaintances, living with grace

These are a few of my gratitude things

Anxiety and depression

When I hear the voice

I simply remember my gratitude things

And know being here's the right choice

Gotta bring Cortney's Place back into the mix. This is a follow-up to their *Too Hot Blues*:

To the tune of The Everly Brothers' *Bye Bye Love*:

There goes my wheelchair, it's melting again
This place is a sauna, messing with my Zen
I'm tired of burning and being hot
It's time for cooling and leaves to fall
Bye bye, heat. Bye bye, sweatiness
Hello, chilly-ness. Bye bye, summer, bye bye
Dehydration makes me cry

The rest of these parodies were written and sung with my courageous behavioral health patients. The following verses were created with a fill-in-the-blank worksheet, which generated the lyrics of multiple verses to the tune of Bob Dylan's/Joan Baez's *Blowin' in the Wind*:

How many pills must I take in a day before I don't want to eat anymore?
How many times must I look in the mirror before I don't think I'm rotten to the core?
How many years will I starve myself before I like what I see?
The answer, my friend, is with more self-esteem.
The answer is more self-esteem.

How many times must I cut myself before I feel the pain?
How many years must I feel empty before I can be alive?
How many years must I hate myself before I learn to love myself?
The answer, my friend, is love and happiness.
The answer is love and happiness.

How many times must I wash my hands before I think they are clean?

How many times must I worry about dirt before I can just let it go?

How many times must I feel anxious before I can handle bacteria?

The answer, my friend, is to learn more coping skills.

The answer is with more coping skills.

How many times will I put myself down before I can see what they see?

How many years must I find good in others before I can find it in me?

How many times must I hear before I believe when they say, "You are all of these things"?

The answer, my friend, is right inside.

The answer is inside of me.

How many substances must I poison myself with before they take my life away?

How many times must I hurt my family before they give up on me?

How many years must I live my life this way before it's time to grow up?

The answer, my friend, is never looking back.

The answer is to never look back.

How many lines must I snort today before I feel okay?

How many times must I blow my nose before I can't smell a frickin' thing?

How many years must I go insane before I can finally be awake?

The answer, my friend, is to leave my old friends.

The answer is to leave my toxic friends.

How many years must I smoke cigarettes before I die before my time?

How many times must I wheeze in the wind before I die of suffocation?

How many puffs must I contribute to pollution before I'm satisfied?

The answer, my friend, is the 4 mg. gum.

The answer is the 4 mg. gum.

Here are a couple silly verses that I wrote and shared to break the ice with patients:

(This is about how I went ukuloco during COVID-19.)

How many ukuleles must I buy before I break the bank?

How much cash must I blow away before I can call myself a pro?

How many hours must I practice on these things before I sound like I spend?

The answer, my friend, is in the uke design.

The answer is how well I play.

(A Christmas verse)

How many light bulbs must crap out on me before I lose my damn mind?

How many rolls of tape must I deplete before I switch to gift bags?

How many cookies must I burn to a crisp before I just buy them at the store?

The answer, my friend, is to keep my sense of humor.

The answer is to use my coping skills.

Alanis Morissette's *Hand in My Pocket* is another good one for this population. We first analyze the original lyrics, where patients share what lyrics resonate with them (including the *dialecticals*—two seemingly opposite things that are true at once), experiences, and insights. We then collectively write new verses with contributions from the group. These are some of my favorites:

I'm sick, but I'm stable
I'm lost, but have hope
Confused, but I'm trying, yeah
I'm down, but I'm giggling
I'm a coward, but I got this
Wiped out, but I'm restless, baby
What it all comes down to
Is that I'm still alive
I got one hand in my pocket
And the other one is reaching out for help

I feel worthless, but I'm honest
I'm lazy, but responsible
I'm shy, but I'm strong, yeah
I'm rough, but I'm roses
I'm violent, but I'm caring
I'm asleep, but I still love you, baby
What it all comes down to
Is that I'm gold and rich at heart
I got one hand in my pocket
And the other one is throwing deuces

I'm homeless, but happy

I'm anxious, but calm

I'm stressed, but optimistic, yeah

I'm tired, but I'm awake

I'm sleeping, but I'm here

I'm poor, but I'm living, baby

And what it all comes down to

Is that I'm trying to live a peaceful life

I got one hand in my pocket

And the other is waving hello, world

My final parody songwriting exercise to share with you utilizes Jana Stanfield's *Nothin' I Can Do About It Now*. If you have not heard of Jana, please look her up. She's an inspirational singer-songwriter with "heavy mental" lyrics. This song epitomizes the essential coping mechanism of being able to laugh at yourself. We are all human and we all do dopey things. Laugh and learn. Here are Jana's original lyrics:

**NOTHIN' I CAN DO ABOUT IT NOW**

At first it seemed so harmless, like most dares in high school are

Pale cheeks against the window in the back seat of the car

It seemed like something everyone should do just once in life

Until I saw that I just mooned our preacher and his wife

**CHORUS:**

**Well, there's nothin' I can do about it now**

**Nothin' I can do about it now**

**Nothin' I can do, nothin' I can do**

**Nothin' I can do about it now**

I ran into a woman I hadn't seen for quite a while
It was clear that any minute, she'd give birth to her next child
So I said, "Congratulations, when's your baby due?"
She said, "Jana, get your glasses checked. The baby's almost two."

CHORUS

I wrote a funny e-mail to my closest friend at work
About a certain customer who can be quite a jerk
The boss came in next morning with the e-mail in his fist
It seems I'd sent it out to our entire client list

CHORUS

So I'm standing at the pearly gates not having any fun
As St. Peter watches videos of all I've said and done
I hope God not only will forgive, but also can forget
Though the way St. Peter's laughing, I'm not placing any bets

CHORUS

The next verse is my personal contribution. This really happened to me when I was a senior in high school.

One sunny day in August, we headed for the lake
I couldn't get up on my skis, kept falling in the wake
After about a million tries, my friends still cheered me on
I was up, but I looked down, my bikini top was gone

CHORUS

The remaining verses were written in my behavioral health groups:

One night not long ago, I was partyin' with friends

The conversation went downhill, the night was comin' to an end

I tried to kick it up a notch, I jumped right in to dance

But I got up too fast and then my drink was in my pants

CHORUS

I was at the county fair, watching bulls ride all over the place

I shot a big snot rocket, it ricocheted in my face

Lucky me, a spectator had caught it all on tape

I ended up on the news, this is a homecoming queen's fate

CHORUS

When I was in the fourth grade, I really had to fart

The teacher was reading a story, she got to an interesting part

I thought I had an opportunity while she kept reading on

I let it go, but she got quiet, and everyone heard my bomb

CHORUS

We were playing Texas Hold 'Em at Huntington Beach

Thoughts of winning this game became quickly out of reach

I lost the game, my punishment involved a pink tutu

As I ran down the beach and yelled, "I'm a pretty princess in the nude!"

CHORUS

On the apartment patio, Thanksgiving, I was eight

We were all just hanging out after finishing our plate

As I walked out, the coast looked clear, but I was very wrong

I crashed into the screen, learned that the door was closed all along

CHORUS

When I met my to-be mother-in-law, she interrogated me about my life

My soon-to-be hubby wanted to introduce me as his wife

He was about to be deployed, by the way, I was his boss

Surprise for Mom, we eloped, she's still a little lost

CHORUS

My mom is four-eleven and her friends are very small

We used words like midget, bobbin' hobbits and Gandalf

Turns out I was overheard by all Mom's tiny friends

Mom told me to please shut up, she almost whipped my rear end

CHORUS

I was on my cycle, getting on a train

Sometimes it sucks to be a girl, the cramps were causing pain

Came back from the bathroom and then I took my seat

My cousin pointed out I had a pad on my right butt-cheek

CHORUS

Playing soccer in third grade, having too much fun

Went after the same ball as him, tripped over my own legs, so dumb

Suddenly I was on the ground and I was seeing stars

It was like an out-of-body experience, I ended up on Mars

CHORUS

When I was in the fifth grade and we were all in class

Everything was going fine 'til I fell on my ass

I stuck my head into a hole and I couldn't move

So they had to call for help and cut the chair in two

CHORUS

My dad got a new pair of pants, but he had lost some weight

The new pants were too big, I guess that was his fate

He was halfway up the stairs when they just fell right down

He tugged 'em up, ran so fast, and took off with a frown

CHORUS

Hanging at Castles & Coasters when I was nine years old

Saw a really cool ride, was feeling kinda bold

The free fall dropped down several times and then I took a glance

There was liquid on the ground 'cus I had peed my pants

CHORUS

About an hour after one of these groups, I was on a unit when a patient who had attended an earlier group knocked over a pitcher and spilled water all over the floor. She paused, put her hands palms up and sang, "Well, there's nothin' I can do about it now…"! One of my prouder moments.

You have read through many examples of simple songwriting. Feeling a little more confident? Remember what I said about keeping it simple. If a Grammy is your goal, you don't get it. Write for you, using new lyrics to ripped-off songs, original music and lyrics, and anything in between and beyond. You can do this!

Let's shift to the funky hippie and final part of this DIY chapter. Energy. Vibration. Sound healing. I'm talking chakras and how to target them through humming, toning, and singing bowls. As with most music, you can prescribe this for yourself at a rudimentary level. Another caution: this is another area where one might attempt to experiment outside their scope of practice. Sound and energy healers have advanced education and training. Schedule a bowl session for deeper work. I'll hook you up.

Toning and humming are effective ways to get in touch with your body and emotions, release tension, center yourself, lower blood pressure, charge your brain, and stimulate bone conduction. Different vowel sounds are used to stimulate different areas of the body. For example, "Ah" helps the chest area to resonate and "Eee" resonates the head and skull (try "Eee" when you're getting drowsy behind the wheel!). If tension exists in these areas, it may be appropriate to tone (resonate) each area to stimulate release. A deep breath or simple sigh can put you back in your body when you feel disconnected or too much in your head. There are many ways to use your voice and breath to support yourself.

- "Eee" resonates in the head
- "Ooo" resonates in the mouth, lips, and face
- "Aye" resonates in the throat
- "Ah" resonates in the chest

- "Oh" resonates the whole body, specifically the gut

That's the toning part. Humming begins as a tone, on a vowel, but closes in on the "m" consonant.

- "Ohm" vibrates in the head
- "Owm" vibrates in the face
- "Huhm" vibrates in the throat
- "Yuhm" vibrates in the chest
- "Ruhm" (roll "r") vibrates in the diaphragm/solar plexus area
- "Vuhm" vibrates in the gut
- "Luhm" vibrates in the pelvic area/base of the spine

Consider how everything in and of our universe is in a constant state of vibration, including our bodies. Isn't it reasonable to correlate a lack of vibration—or blocked vibration—with illness, disease, and dysfunction? We can actually target blocked vibration with sound.

The seven chakras are the energy centers of our bodies. The word *chakra* is Sanskrit for wheel or disk, and signifies one of seven basic energy centers in the body. Each of these centers corresponds to major nerve ganglia branching forth from the spinal column. Chakras also parallel levels of consciousness, archetypal elements, developmental stages of life, colors, sounds, body functions, and much more. From the top down:

## SEVENTH CHAKRA (CROWN)

Location: Head/Cerebral Plexus

Association: Knowledge, wisdom, understanding, cosmic awareness, spiritual connection, consciousness, thought, bliss

Corresponding Color: Violet

Musical Note: B

Humming Vowel: "Ohm"

## SIXTH CHAKRA *(THIRD EYE)*

Location: Center of Forehead

Association: Self-realization, intuition, understanding, visualization, inner vision, light, archetypal identity, self-reflection, seeing physically and intuitively

Corresponding Color: Dark Indigo Blue

Musical Note: A

Humming Vowel: "Owm"

## FIFTH CHAKRA *(THROAT)*

Location: Base of Throat

Association: Communication, creativity, expression, sound, language, speaking one's truth

Corresponding Color: Azure Blue

Musical Note: G

Humming Vowel: "Huhm"

## FOURTH CHAKRA (HEART)

Location: Center of Chest, even with nipple line

Association: Air, sense of balance and peace, compassion, friendship, empathy, the ability to give and receive love, social identity, self-acceptance, ego, unity

Corresponding Color: Green

Musical Note: F

Humming Vowel: "Yuhm"

## THIRD CHAKRA *(SOLAR PLEXUS)*

Location: Midway between the end of the breastbone and the navel

Association: Fire, ego, emotions (including blocked emotions), identity, will, personal power, autonomy, passion for living, the ability to protect oneself from being the target of negative or aggressive emotions, metabolism, energy, effectiveness, spontaneity

Corresponding Color: Yellow

Musical Note: E

Humming Vowel: "Ruhm" (roll "R")

## SECOND CHAKRA *(SACRAL)*

Location: Genitals/sexual organs

Association: Water, sexuality, desire, sensation, relationships, reproduction, serendipity, emotional identity, self-gratification, movement, fluidity, grace, depth of feeling, change

Corresponding Color: Orange

Musical Note: D

Humming Vowel: "Vuhm"

## FIRST CHAKRA *(ROOT)*

Location: Base of spine

Association: Earth, security, self-preservation, health, prosperity, survival, drive, ambition, grounding one's energy in the physical dimension, life forces, physical identity, foundation, grounding, health, prosperity, security, dynamic presence

Corresponding Color: Red

Musical Note: C

Humming Vowel: "Luhm"

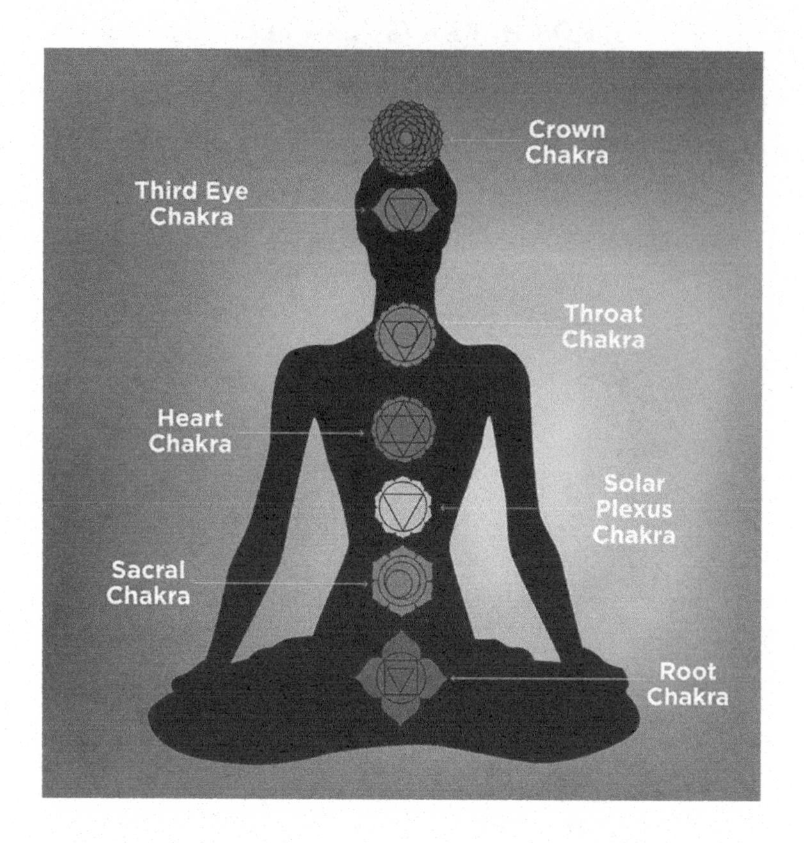


Use your voice to vibrate a targeted chakra and potentially release its blocked energy. Another instrument for energy work is the Tibetan singing bowl. Use the B-pitched bowl for the crown chakra (seventh) when you need to clear your head. Use the E bowl for the solar plexus chakra (third) to release blocked emotions. Use the C bowl for the root chakra (first) if you need grounding or a stronger sense of security. Use the G bowl to target the throat chakra (fifth) to prepare yourself for an uncomfortable conversation. Use the corresponding bowl to unblock any area of your body that is compromised, damaged, or diseased.

Singing bowls were brought to Tibet from India with the teachings of Buddha. They are hammered by hand in a combination of seven native Himalayan metals, which create seven distinct tones. The seven metals correspond with each of the planets: gold for the Sun, silver for the Moon, mercury for, uh, Mercury, copper for Venus, iron for Mars, tin for Jupiter, and lead for Saturn.

Playing the bowl can be tricky. A smaller bowl is held on the palm of your hand. Bigger and heavier bowls can remain on a cushion on a solid surface. Hold the mallet (wood, felt, or rubber) mid-length with fingertips pointing down and touching the mallet. With even pressure, rub the mallet clockwise around the bowl's outer rim. Use a full arm movement, like stirring a big kettle. Increase the speed as the bowl begins to vibrate and the sound builds. Apply pressure. The friction of the mallet against the outer rim of the bowl produces the vibrations which result in sound. The sound can sustain for a couple minutes.

Crystal bowls are used for similar purposes. They are downright gorgeous. And very expensive. If you've got the coin, you won't be disappointed. I'm too poor for a crystal bowl collection, but I do have a few little Tibetan singing bowls. As with a decent drum, a singing bowl is a small investment for health and wellness.

Purchase or make instruments. Play musical games. Sing. Analyze lyrics. Write music and lyrics. Drum. Target sound and energy. Make playlists. Vibe to all beats. You now have several useful tools in your musical arsenal. This being the penultimate chapter, my work here is nearly done.

# XII. FINALE

*"Drench yourself in words unspoken. Live your life with arms wide open. Today is where your book begins. The rest is still unwritten."*
*—Natasha Bedingfield*

I saw this in a meme: "When the world gets to be too much, when life gets too hard…play more music, listen to more music, practice more music, write more music, just get lost in more music for a while." There was no attribution, so I'm stealing it because it is more or less the message—the chorus—of this book.

You now have a myriad of evidence-based information on music and its therapeutic advantages. Please contemplate a few factors as you begin preparations for the next path in your musical journey. Cultural background, age, and musical preferences should be considered when using music with others, whether it is intended for recreational or therapeutic use.

Music can enhance or alter mood and activity/energy level. When making choices between stimulating and sedative music, use common sense. In general, use upbeat music to arouse a lethargic person; use soft, slow music to calm the anxious, agitated, or overactive person. That person might be you. With live music (as opposed to recorded), we can adjust the energy level, tempo, and/or dynamics to suit the occasion or mood.

Include other senses in the musical experience. I frequently combine music with art, colors, textures, movement, aromas, even tastes (nobody refuses Jolly Ranchers as a prize for Musical Jeopardy; better than braggin' rights). Paint to music. Make collages of inspirational lyrics. Create notecards with positive affirmations and music quotes to leave for yourself around the house...on the bathroom mirror, in a drawer, in a purse or backpack, etc. Music itself is visual and kinesthetic, just as much as it is auditory. I see the music I'm playing, I see the conductor, I see my fellow musicians, I see people listening, responding, and dancing. I caress and breathe in the stunning woods of my stringed instruments. I strum, pluck, and pick. All ten of my fingers touch the eighty-eight keys of a piano. My entire hands, arms, shoulders, and back get a workout drumming.

We music therapists use the iso principle—music's ability to match and alter mood. Research shows that when the mood of music is matched to an individual's present mood and then gradually changed, that person's mood can also be altered (Crowe, 2004). So if you're super amped up and need to decompress, start by listening to something allegro (fast, upbeat) to match where you are in the moment. Next play something to start bringing it down, something andante (moderate tempo). Now shift to adagio (slow, soft) and keep it there. Make sense?

Lastly, consider your own abilities. Challenge yourself, but set yourself up for success. Mistakes (missteps) are allies. As with any form of art, if you don't make a mess, you're not doing it right. Also, if you use music therapeutically with a loved one, be wary of crossing into territory that's beyond your knowledge and training. Music therapy is a legitimate, unique treatment modality. The profession should be recognized and respected as such. One more consideration. How about a career in this celebrated profession?!

I'd like to touch on one more powerful intervention for music therapy, which is also a brilliant performance style and something anyone can do, even at the most fundamental level. Improvisation. Yikes, that's another scary word like songwriting! Well, most creative experiences are both fascinating and terrifying, right? The extraordinary skills of jazz aficionados and the cast of *Whose Line is it Anyway?* are a bit too ambitious for most of us, so no worries. You cannot improvise wrong.

I'm talking about the kind of improvisation that is simply making it up as you go. A spontaneous creation of music and sound. In some cases, there are no rules. In others, ample structure is necessary. Societal and cultural influence may play a role. Instinct is inevitable. Fun times are guaranteed.

Improvisation is much freer and more flexible than playing by ear or playing in a certain style. We can start with playing how we feel or playing the music within. If you're doing this with others, emphasize no judgment as unskilled participants will undoubtedly feel vulnerable.

Music therapy guru, Tony Wigram (2004) explained how improvisation is personal. An individual's past influences on the musical process (and *product*) include the musical culture from which they came, the musical skills they have acquired, musical taste and preferences, influences in the way they have learned music, and associations to the past and life events. Present impacts include current musical fads or interests, culturally influenced life events, mood or emotional state at the time, and personality state and character as they are currently developed. All these elements combine to form a musical identity that surfaces while improvising music.

Wigram suggested creative simplicity as a starting point with the following methods:

- One-note, two-note, three-note, and four-note improvisations
- Improvising on a single chord
- Improvising with just one hand

- Melody improvisation alone (on a pitched instrument...piano or xylophone, for example)
- Simple rhythmic dialogue

Try this non-threatening, simple improvisation, either on your own or with a partner. If you happen to possess and know how to play a Native American flute, improvise on it. Your partner can play a rain stick or an ocean drum, which is a frame drum with tiny steel beads inside. Gently manipulate the drum to roll the beads around to generate the sound of waves. It is a beautiful equalizer to the flute and creates a soothing, tranquil atmosphere. No flute? Carlos Nakai is a two-word search away. Play one of his recordings while you listen, breathe, and contribute with whatever instrument you like. That instrument might be your own body percussion (clapping, snapping, tapping, beatboxing, etc.).

Basic drumming makes for tasty improvisation and may be loosely to highly structured, depending on your intentions. Gather a small group and sit in a circle with your instrument (ideally, there should be at least fifty percent drums and the rest a variety of hand percussion instruments—tambourines, shakers, cabasas, claves, etc.). Play together in rhythm at a moderate tempo, just a simple 1-2-3-4. When everyone seems gelled, go around the circle for each participant to play an eight-count solo over the steady beat. That's one technique. Another is to lay down a simple foundation and then have others come in one at a time, layering new and complementing patterns. You may feel something organic and even cathartic that materializes in these improvised experiences.

Next, find yourself at a piano or keyboard. Play white keys only and see what materializes. You will be playing in C major or A minor (it's all relative, snort!) and can't mess it up. Same concept for playing the black keys only (F# major or D# minor). Depending on your piano skills, you could play an ostinato pattern (a continuously repeated musical rhythm or phrase) on the lower piano keys to support someone else who improvises on the higher piano keys. For example, in the key of C major, you could play a simple I-IV-V (C-F-G) progression while your partner tinkers on the white keys. A boom-chuck-chuck or boogie-woogie/blues pattern can also go a long way. If you are so indomitable, try modal frameworks (Dorian, Aeolian) and world beats (cha-cha, cumbia). Experiment with these rhythms on other instruments.

Try tuning a guitar to D-A-D-F#-A-D (as opposed to the standard E-A-D-G-B-E). Your guitar is now cheater-tuned to the key of D major. Noodle around in solo fashion. Completely cover the fifth fret and you're now playing G major. Completely cover the seventh fret and you're playing A major. With quick movement of one strong finger, you can play D-G-A (I-IV-V) and accompany yourself with a simple up and down strumming pattern.

Depending on how structured you wish to get, occasional directives can be helpful. Wigram (2004) gives the examples of, "Let's start very softly, get extremely loud and then go back to being very soft" and "Let's think of a place where we feel safe and comfortable and play that feeling, and then gradually step outside the door into a dangerous and difficult world. When we start to feel too insecure in our difficult world, let's move back into our nice safe, comfortable space." Dialoguing is another interesting process, where the improvisers communicate through their musical play.

Additional techniques on instruments include exploring the sound, passing a message, musical portrait (of yourself, of your ideal self, of another), echo/call and response, starting one at a time, conducting, and soft-loud-soft. Include voice, movement, and relaxation if it feels right (Wigram, 2004). Improvisations are musical, human, uniting events that embrace creativity, exploration, and personal fulfillment.

I hope you try these activities and find them to be user friendly, practical, and beneficial. Regrets to any music techies out there. I did not include music from a production perspective, mainly because I'm a technology and mechanics dimwit. I am blown away by how far we have come over the last century with recording and playback technology. I just don't have a knack for it. Maybe that's your thing. Editing, sampling, synthesizing, mixing, and more of the behind-the-scenes construction of music. Or does the commercial aspect—marketing and distribution—appeal to you? These are all conceivable complementary areas for musical exploration and adventure.

In closing, I invite you to complete the sentences below about music for self-care (partially borrowed from Christine Stevens, 2012).

**How is music therapeutic for you?**

______________________________________________

**Music inspires me to**

______________________________________________

**When I sing, I**

______________________________________________

**I am a symphony of**

______________________________________________

**Making music with others offers me**

______________________________________________

**My favorite music sends me a message of**

______________________________________________

**If I were an instrument, I would be a**

______________________________________________

**Music motivates me to**

______________________________________________

**My rhythm is**

______________________________________________

**My artist or band name is**

______________________________________________

**The playlist for my day is**

______________________________________________

**The soundtrack of my life is**

______________________________________________

We are approaching the book's curtain call. I have immensely enjoyed compiling bits of history and science with personal and professional chronicles of music's magic to share with you. I feel harmony in my heart and thank you for investing the time and energy into this examination of songs and lyrics.

Three requests: 1) Support local musicians and immerse yourself into the local music scene as a spectator, performer, manager, or venue worker. 2) Consider purchasing complete albums instead the two songs that grabbed you from radio play. An album, back in the days of vinyl, told a story. Would you only read Chapters 4 and 12 of a twenty-chapter book? 3) Diversify your musical interests; embrace the music and lessons other cultures and genres have to offer.

With all that in mind, here is a final exercise to work on at your leisure. Tally the number of songs for *your* album. What is the album title? How many songs tell *your* story? What are the song titles? What does the art look like? Will you write it? Will you sing and play on it? Will you produce it? Will you collaborate? When will you listen to it? Will you share it with others?

I hope my voice has helped you find yours—and use it. You got this. And I got you. An inspiration duet of sorts. So...*Build Me Up, Buttercup* (The Foundations). I'll gladly reciprocate. Time to start music-ing!

Make the most of this musical existence. Live out loud. Cultivate connections. Breathe for grounding. Hum loose a blocked chakra. Sing on a rooftop. Dance on the table. Crash a wedding reception and play tambourine with the band. Cry at the opera. Treat yourself to a sound bath with Chopin and engage all your senses as you tap into the imagery of nature and beauty. Make mistakes. Make 'em loud. Own them, honor them, and then let it go and move forward. Accuracy is far less important than the therapeutic value of just doing music.

Whatever you're experiencing, dealing with, learning, celebrating... pour some music on it. Live, laugh, love music. I bet there's a song for that.

Dave Cruz, Photographer

# XIII. ENCORE (GRATITUDE AND ACKNOWLEDGEMENTS)

*"So here I go, it's my shot. Feet fail me not. This may be the only opportunity that I got." —Eminem*

I wanted to write a book my entire adult life. I had some thoughts, outlines, and chapter attempts that never really amounted to much because it was a side thing. When COVID-19 hit in 2020, I experienced work changes that involved new challenges, adventures, and rewards. It was around this time that my mind became restless and another writing project started percolating.

Remember when I told you about the reflexology massage and how my cerebral musings collided in a ruminating anagram to structure my tendrils of ideas? Probably not coincidentally, that same day, I finished my dear friend and co-conspirator in badassery, Kristina Paider's book, *The Hollywood Approach: Script Your Life Like a Hit Movie and Live Your Wildest Dream*. Kristina wrote about the antagonists that get in the way of making a dream a reality. I took inventory of the obstacles standing between me and bringing this book idea to fruition. Time was my biggest, greediest antagonist. The programmed limitations from my stretch in the world of academia, also an antagonist. Justifying what might seem like an indulgence to some, writing about my life and accomplishments, and assuming people could give a crap. The antagonists kept clambering out of every crevice in my physical and mental environment. Thank you, Kristina, for kicking me in the butt. You inspired me to abandon all the antagonists. I haven't looked back.

Never-ending squeezes to my sweet babies (not babies anymore), Dylan and Kaylee Murillo. They witnessed much of my music therapy work and assisted in my groups when they were younger, dancing with developmentally disabled adults and helping them play instruments. They are abundantly talented and compassionate. They know first-hand how music can connect people and serve as a tool for learning, coping, and change.

Shout-out to my moms, Sheila Hoffer and Mary Pendleton-Hoffer, who have had a prominent musical presence in my life as long as I can remember. I wish my dad, Warren Hoffer, could read this. He was a strong advocate for music therapy and one of my biggest musical influences. Gratitude extends to my entire immediate family: Michael Hoffer and company, Jonathan Hoffer, et al., Howard Weinstein, and Jim Meador.

Thanks to the hundreds—maybe thousands—of people I have made music with over the years, but most specifically, Meri Levy, Carolyn Kimball, Jennie Evashenko, Chris Cahoon, Steve Wells, Michael Dollin, Dan Spencer, Jim Hall, and Tim Layman (plus all you "occasionals" and guests!).

Thank you to the influential instructors who shaped my skill set and my practice, including Barbara Crowe, Robin Rio, and Judy May. Hugs to my extended music therapy family of beautiful human beans and its concentric circles of colleagues: Debi Kret, Frank Thompson, Kymla Eubanks, Lisa Sampson, Sally Niles, Dalena Watson, Jane Shallberg, Jodi Richardson-Delgado, Danielle Franklin, Annamaria Oliverio, Stephanie Bianchi, Kay Norton, George Umberson, Jere Humphreys, Marc Wilson, Trudy Gomez, Stephanie Rozner, Katie Sample, Adrian Romero, and Cami Turley.

My music therapy students always brought me tremendous stimulation, motivation, and satisfaction. I feel blessed to have maintained so many relationships with them over the years.

Thank you to my clients/patients, specifically, any subjects of and participants in my research (whose names have been changed to protect anonymity). You are my ultimate inspiration.

I would like to acknowledge my publishing team at BookBaby for their professional support with editing, design, marketing, and distribution.

My mantra then and now: "We are in this line of work not for the income, but for the outcome." The positive outcomes I have witnessed in my music therapy work make me a very rich individual indeed. My eternal hope is that music will continue to unite and promote learning and healing.

To you, the reader, I wish you abundant blessings through music. May your life crescendo with joy every day.

# BIBLIOGRAPHY

Abeles, H.F. (1980). Responses to music. In D.A. Hodges (Ed.), *Handbook of music psychology* (pp. 105-140) Lawrence: National Association for Music Therapy.

AC/DC. (1981). For Those About to Rock (We Salute You) [Song]. On *Who Made Who*. Albert Productions.

Ainsley, R., (Ed.) (1999). *The encyclopedia of classical music*. London: Carlton Books.

American Music Therapy Association. (2021). Retrieved from http://www.musictherapy.org.

American Psychiatric Association. (2013). *Diagnostic and statistical manual of mental disorders: DSM-V-TR*. Washington, DC: American Psychiatric Association.

Ansdell, G. (2004). Rethinking music and community: theoretical perspectives in support of community music therapy. In Pavlicevic, M. & Ansdell, G. (Eds.) *Community music therapy* (pp. 65-90). London: Jessica Kingsley Publishers.

Armstrong, L. (1994). What a Wonderful World [Song]. On *Louis Armstrong's All Time Greatest Hits*. Geffen Records.

Ashida, S. (2000). The effect of reminiscence music therapy sessions on changes in depressive symptoms in elderly persons with dementia. *Journal of Music Therapy*, *38* (3), 170-182.

Bedingfield, N. (2004). Unwritten [Song]. On *Natasha Bedingfield.* Phonogenic Records.

Biller, J.D., Olson, P.J., & Green, T. (1974). The effect of "happy" versus "sad" music and participation on anxiety. *Journal of Music Therapy, 11*, Summer, 68-73.

Bitcom, C. (1981). Guest editorial. *Journal of Music Therapy, 18*, 2-6.

Boltz, M.G. (1998). Tempo discrimination of musical patterns: Effects due to pitch and rhythmic structure. *Perception and Psychophysics, 60* (8), 1,357-1,373.

Brown, N.B. & Bruce, S.E. (2016). Stigma, Career Worry, and Mental Illness Symptomatology: Factors Influencing Treatment-Seeking for Operation Enduring Freedom and Operation Iraqi Freedom Soldiers and Veterans. *Psychological trauma: Theory, research, practice, and policy, 3*, 276-283.

Bruscia, K.E. (1998). *Defining music therapy.* Gilsum: Barcelona Publishers.

Cassity, M.D. & Cassity, J.E. (1998). *Multimodal psychiatric music therapy for adults, adolescents, and children: a clinical manual.* St. Louis: MMB Music.

Certification Board for Music Therapists. (2021). Retrieved from http://www.cbmt.org/about/.

Cherniss, C. (1980). *Job stress in the human services.* Beverly Hills, CA; London: Sage Publications. cmap. (2021). Retrieved from Evolution+of+American+Music+Genres.cmap(970x574)(ihmc.us).

Commander Cody and His Lost Planet Airmen (2013). Smoke! Smoke! Smoke! (That Cigarette) [Song]. On *Hot to Trot.* Akarma Records.

Conrad, P.L., Young, C., Hogan, L., & Armstrong, M.L. (2014). Encountering women veterans with military sexual trauma. *Perspectives in Psychiatric Care, 50*, 280-286.

Cooke, S. (2000). What a Wonderful World [Song]. On *The Man Who Invented Soul.* RCA/Victor.

Cordobes, T.K. (1997). Group songwriting as a method for developing group cohesion for HIV-seropositive adult patients with depression. *Journal of Music Therapy, 34* (1), 46-67.

Cotton, D.H.G. (1990). *Stress management: An integrated approach to therapy.* New York: Brunner/Mazel.

Croal, N. (2001). Music: Ladies with attitude. *Newsweek,* 19. <http://archives.newsbank.com/arsearch/we/Archives?p_action=doc&p_docid=0EDA52D0D105BA46&p_docnum=68&s_accounted+AC0103072017554403910&s_orderid=B-B0103072017552503864&s_dlid =DL0103072017564504019&s.

Crowe, B.J. (2004). *Music and soulmaking: Toward a new theory of music therapy.* Lanham, MD: Scarecrow Press, Inc.

Danton, E. (2002). Can girls save rock 'n roll? Not while their lip gloss gets more attention than their guitar licks." *Sydney Morning Herald.* <http://www.smh.com.au/handheld/articles/2001/01/02/1041196742936.htm>.

Davis, W.B., Gfeller, K.E., & Thaut, M.H. (1999). *An introduction to music therapy theory and practice.* Boston: McGraw-Hill.

Digital Music News. (2021). Retrieved from genre_breakdown_2015_2.png(657x654)(digitalmusicnews.com).

Eminem. (2002). Lose Yourself [Song]. On *8 Mile.* Shady Records.

Epstein, D. (1993). On affect and musical motion. In S. Feder, R.L. Karmel & G.H. Pollock (Eds.), *Psychoanalytic explorations in music* (pp. 91-123). Madison: International Universities.

Erickson, E. (1963). *Childhood and society* (2nd ed.). New York: Norton.

Figley, C. (1995). Compassion fatigue: Toward a new understanding of the costs of caring. In B.H. Stamm (Ed.), *Secondary traumatic stress: Self-care issues for clinicians, researchers, and educators* (pp. 3-29). Lutherville: Sidran.

Florida Georgia Line. (2016). Music is Healing [Song]. On *Dig Your Roots*. Big Machine Label Group.

Forinash, M. (Ed.). (2001). *Music therapy supervision*. Gilsum, H.: Barcelona Publishers.

Fowler, K.L. (2006). The relationship between personality characteristics, work environment, and the professional well-being of music therapists. *Journal of Music Therapy, 43* (3), 174-197.

Freudenberger, H. (1974). Staff burn-out. *Journal of Social Issues, 30* (1), 159-164.

Gaar, G. (2002). *She's A rebel: The history of women in rock & roll*. New York: Seal Press.

Gabriel, P. (2010). Book of Love [Song]. On *Scratch My Back*. Virgin Records.

Goins, W.E. (1998). The effect of moodstates: Continuous versus summative responses. Journal of Music Therapy, 35 (4), 242-258.

Green, C. (2010). Fuck You [Song]. On *The Lady Killer*. Elektra Records.

Greenberg, D.M., et al. (2021). The social neuroscience of music: Understanding the social brain through human song. Retrieved from https://medicalxpress.com/news/2021-06-brain-people-music.html.

Greenberg, J.S. (2002). Comprehensive stress management (7th ed.). Boston: McGraw – Hill. Haack, P.A. (1980). The behavior of music listeners. In D. Hodges (Ed.), *Handbook of music psychology* (pp. 141-182). Lawrence: National Association for Music Therapy.

Greenday. (1997). Good Riddance (Time of Your Life) [Song]. On *Nimrod*. Reprise Records.

Hanser, S. (2018). *The new music therapist's handbook*, 3rd Ed. Boston, MA: Berklee Press.

Higgins, K.M. (1997). Musical idiosyncrasy and perspectival listening. In J. Robinson (Ed.), *Music and meaning* (pp. 83-102). Ithaca and London: Cornell University.

Hirshey, G. (2001). *We gotta get out of this place: The true, tough story of women in rock.* New York: Grove Press.

Hodges, D.A. (1980). Appendix A: physiological responses to music. In D.A. Hodges (Ed.), *Handbook of music psychology* (pp. 393-400). Lawrence: National Association for Music Therapy.

Hoffer-Murillo, J. (2013). *A survey of board-certified music therapists: perceptions of the profession, the impact of stress and burnout, and the need for self-care.* Ann Arbor, MI: ProQuest, LLC.

Isley Brothers. (2016). It's Your Thing [Song]. On *It's Your Thing.* T-Neck Records.

Jaffe, D.T., & Scott, C.D. (1984). *From burnout to balance.* New York: McGraw-Hill Book Company.

Joel, B. (1989). We Didn't Start the Fire [Song]. On *Storm Front.* Columbia Records.

Jourdain, R. (1997). *Music, the brain, and ecstasy.* New York: Avon.

Knoll, Reuer, B., & Henry, D. (1988). Working ways: Tips for job success. *Music Therapy Perspectives, 5*, 119-120.

Leon, A.M., Altholz, J.A.S., & Dziegielewski, S.F. (1999). Compassion fatigue: Considerations for working with the elderly. *Journal of Gerontological Social Work, 32* (1): 43-62.

Lester, N. (2010). Compassion fatigue. *Mental Health Practice, 14* (2), 11.

Levinson, J. (1997). Music and negative emotion. In J. Robinson (Ed.), *Music and meaning* (pp. 215-241). Ithaca and London: Cornell University.

Liveaboutmusic. (2021). Retrieved from *A beginner's guide to music history* (liveabout.com).

Maher, E.L. (1983). Burnout and commitment: A theoretical alternative. *Personnel and Guidance, 61*, 390-393.

Mathis, J. (2004). The 12th of Never [Song]. On *The Essential Johnny Mathis.* Columbia Records.

Martin, J.A. (1991). Music therapy at the end of a life. In Bruscia, K.E. (Ed.) *Case studies in music therapy* (pp. 617-632). Gilsum, NH: Barcelona Publishers.

Maslach, C. (1976). Burned out. *Human Behavior, 5* (9), 16-22.

McInnis-Dittrich, K. (2009). *Social work with older adults: A biopsychosocial approach to assessment and intervention.* Boston: Pearson Education, Inc.

McInnish-Dittrich, K. (2009). *Social work with older adults* (3rd ed.). Boston: Pearson Education, Inc.

Merriam-Webster Dictionary. (2013) Retrieved from http://www.merriam-webster.com/ dictionary/burnout.

Migliore, M.J. (1991). The Hamilton rating scale for depression and rhythmic competency: A correlational study. *Journal of Music Therapy, 28* (4), 211-221.

Morrison, J. (1994). Complete DSM-IV criteria for mental disorders, replicated from *DSM-IV made easy.* Retrieved October 5, 2002, from http://www.geocities.com/morrison94/index.htm.

Mraz, J. (2008). I'm Yours [Song]. On *We Sing. We Dance. We Steal Things.* Atlantic Records.

National Association for Music Education. (2021). Retrieved from http://www.nafme.org

Norman, R. (2009). *The relationship between music therapists' personal use of music and work engagement.* Unpublished master's thesis, Saint Mary-of-the-Woods College, Saint Mary-of-the-Woods.

Northcut, T.B. & Kienow, A. (2014). The trauma trifecta of military sexual trauma: A case study illustrating the integration of mind and body in clinical work with survivors of MST. *Clinical Social Work, 42,* 247-259.

Norton, K. (2016). *Singing and wellbeing: Ancient wisdom, modern proof.* New York, NY: Routledge Taylor & Francis Group.

Noy, P. (1993). How music conveys emotion. In S. Feder, R.L. Karmel & G.H. Pollock (Eds.), *Psychoanalytic explorations in music* (pp. 125-149). Madison: International Universities.

Okun, B.F. (2002). *Effective helping: Interviewing and counseling techniques.* Pacific Grove, CA: Brooks/Cole.

Oppenheim, L. (1987). Factors related to occupational stress or burnout among music therapists. *Journal of Music Therapy, 24* (2), 97-106.

Ostwald, P.F. (1966). Music and human emotions—discussion. *Journal of Music Therapy, 3* (3), 93-94.

Peters, J.S. (1987). *Music therapy, an introduction.* Springfield: Thomas Books.

Pines, A. & Kafry, D. (1978). Occupational tedium in the social services. *Social Work, 23* (6), 499-507.

Plach, T. (1996). *The creative use of music in group therapy.* Springfield: Thomas Books.

Predictive Safety. (2021). Retrieved from http://www.predictivesafety.coom/blog/the-7-types-of-memory-and-how-to-improve-them.

Radocy, R.E. & Boyle, J.D. (1988). *Psychological foundations of musical behavior* (2nd edition). Springfield: Thomas.

Rodgers, R. & Hammerstein, O. (2018). You'll Never Walk Alone [Song]. On *Carousel 2018 Broadway Cast Recording.* Craft Recordings.

Rose, G.J. (1993). On form and feeling in music. In S. Feder, R.L. Karmel, & G.H. Pollock (Eds.), *Psychoanalytic explorations in music* (pp. 63-81). Madison: International Universities.

Rowe, M.M. (1999). Teaching health-care providers coping: Results of a two-year study. *Journal of Behavioral Medicine, 22,* 511-527.

Sacks, O. (2007). *Musicophilia: Tales of music and the brain.* New York, NY: Alfred A. Knoff, Inc.

Salmon, D. & Stewart, K. (2005). The role of music therapy in care for the caregivers of the terminally ill. In C. Dileo & J.V. Loewy (Eds.) *Music therapy at the end of life* (pp. 239-250). Cherry Hill, NJ: Jeffrey Books.

Scheirer, E.D. (1998). Tempo and beat analysis of acoustic musical signals. *The Journal of the Acoustical Society of America, 103* (1), 588-601.

Schingle, J. C. (2009). A disparate impact on female veterans: The unintended consequences of VA regulations governing the burdens of proof for Post-Traumatic Stress Disorder due to combat and military sexual trauma. *SSRN Electronic Journal SSRN Journal, 16* (1), 6th ser., 155-177.

Seraphine, P. (2021). Retrieved from http://www.NeuroDrumming.com.

Simplicable. (2021). Retrieved from http://www.simplicable.com/new/tradition.

Skaine, R. (2016). *Sexual assault in the U.S. military: The battle within America's armed forces.* Praeger Security International.

Skjelsbaek, I. (2001). Sexual violence and war: Mapping out a complex relationship. *European Journal of International Relations, 7* (2), 211-237.

Smith, R.J., & Steindler, E.M. (1983). The impact of difficult patients upon treaters: Consequences and remedies. *Bulletin of the Menninger Clinic, 47* (2), 107-116.

Softschools. (2021). Retrieved from Music genres timeline (softschools.com).

Spicuzza, F. & Devoe, M. (1982). Burnout in the helping professions: Mutual aid groups as self-help. *Personnel and Guidance, 61*, 95-99.

Stanfield, J. (2003). Nothing I Can Do About it Now [Song]. On *Let the Change Begin, Vol. 4.* Relatively Famous Records.

Stevens, C. (2012). *Music medicine: the science and spirit of healing yourself with sound.* Boulder, CO; Sounds True, Inc.

Stratton, V.N. & Zalanowski, A.H. (1997). The relationship between characteristic moods and most commonly listened to types of music. *Journal of Music Therapy, 34* (2), 129-140.

Suris, A., & Lind, L. (2008). Military sexual trauma: A review of prevalence and associated health consequences in veterans. *Trauma, violence, & abuse, 9* (4), 250-269.

Swezey, S.C. (2013). *What keeps us well? Professional quality of life and career sustaining behaviors of music therapy professionals.* Unpublished master's thesis, University of Kentucky, Lexington.

The People History. (2021). Retrieved from Music history including genres styles, bands and artists over 90 years (thepeoplehistory.com).

Turchek, J. A. & Wilson, S.M. (2010). Sexual assault in the U.S. military: A review of the literature and recommendations for the future. *Aggression and Violent Behavior, 15*, 267-277.

United States Department of Veteran Affairs. (2015). Retrieved from https://www.ptsd.va.gov/understand/types/sexual_trauma_military.asp.

U.S. Department of Veterans Affairs National Center for PTSD. (2015). Retrieved from http://www.ptsd.va.gov/public/types/violence/military-sexual-trauma-general.asp.

Valent, P. (1995). Survival strategies: A framework for understanding secondary traumatic stress and coping in helpers. In C.R. Figley (Ed)., *Compassion fatigue: Coping with secondary traumatic stress disorder in those who treat the traumatized* (pp. 21-50), New York: Brunner/Mazel.

Vega, V.P. (2010). Personality, burnout, and longevity among professional music therapists. *Journal of Music Therapy, 47* (2), 155-179.

Very Well Mind. (2021). Retrieved from http://www.verywellmind.com/an-overview-of-the-types-of-emotions-4163976.

Walton, K. (1997). Listening with imagination: Is music representational? In J. Robinson (Ed.), *Music and Meaning* (pp. 57-82). Ithaca and London: Cornell University.

Wigram, T. & DeBacker, J. (1999). *Clinical applications of music therapy in psychiatry.* London and Philadelphia: Jessica Kingsley Publishers.

Wigram T. (2004). *Improvisation: Methods and techniques for music therapy clinicians, educators and students.* London and Philadelphia: Jessica Kingsley Publishers.

Wyeth, L. (2018). Retrieved from Timeline of musical styles & guitar history, acousticmusic.org.

Youngbloods. (2002). Get Together [Song]. On *Get Together: The Essential Youngbloods.* BMG Heritage/RCA.

Zimney, G.H. (1961). Physiological effects of music. *Music Therapy 1961, 11*, 183-188.

Zippia. (2021). Music therapist demographics and statistics in the US. Retrieved August 14, 2021, from http://www.zippia.com/music-therapist-jobs/demographics/.

# ABOUT THE AUTHOR

Dave Cruz, Photographer

Julie Hoffer, MM, MT-BC, has been a Board-Certified Music Therapist since 2005. She strategically utilizes music as the catalyst for therapeutic interaction to address psychosocial, cognitive, physical, communicative, and spiritual needs, helping individuals attain and maintain maximum levels of functioning. Ms. Hoffer has diverse, multicultural clinical experience with nearly all populations and settings including medical/hospital, hospice, behavioral health, geriatrics, brain injury, developmental disabilities, and wellness. Ms. Hoffer was a clinical professor of music therapy at Arizona State University for nine years, where she coordinated student placements for fieldwork and taught undergraduate and graduate courses in the areas of practicum, music competencies (voice, guitar, piano, percussion), music therapy repertoire, children's music, psychology/neurology of music, basic counseling skills, improvisation, professional writing, and music therapy marketing. Ms. Hoffer holds a Master of Music degree in Music Therapy from Arizona State University and a Post-Graduate Bachelor of Music degree in Music Therapy from Arizona State University, as well as a Bachelor of Science degree in Communications from Northern Arizona University. She has two children and resides in Tempe, Arizona. She hopes to retire as a singing gondola sailor in Venice, Italy.

www.juliehoffer.com